THE ETRUSCANS

A new investigation

Echoes of the Ancient World

THE ETRUSCANS

A new investigation

Mauro Cristofani

translated by
BRIAN PHILLIPS
photographs by
MARIO CARRIERI

Galahad Books · New York City

Designed by Roberto Maderna
Line-drawings and maps by Studio Russo
Title page: Rear wall of the Tomb of the Augurs (Tarquinia 540 – 520 BC)
50125

CONTENTS

Mauro Cristofani and the Publishers would like to thank the staff of the museums which permitted the
photography in this book, and in particular they would like to acknowledge the help of the town councils
of Grosseto, Piacenza, Rome, and Siena; The Trust for the administration of the Guarnacci Museum
and Library, Volterra; The Vatican Museum; The Museum of the Etruscan Academy, Cortona; The
Department of Etrurian Archaeology, Florence; The Department of Southern Etrurian Archaeology,
Rome; and the Department of Umbrian Archaeology, Perugia.

Mario Carrieri and the Publishers would like to thank the heirs of the Torlonia family for their kind
permission to use the photographs on pages 82, 85 and 94.

Preface

This is a book with pictures, and some of the pictures are very beautiful. But Professor Cristofani's essay is not just another picture book about the Etruscans. On the contrary: it is a leading scholar's account of his subject, written in Italy for the general public whose taxes pay for the research here described and evaluated. And it is immediately apparent from the list of Contents that this is a 'different' book about the Etruscans: the traditional first chapter on the non-problem of origins is at last assigned to its proper place – two pages at the end, so that there is more space for the real problems and their solutions.

The combination of readability and reliability in the pages that follow will come as no surprise to those who are already acquainted with Professor Cristofani's professional contributions to his subject. They range in scope from an incisive assessment of the new functional and structural approaches now indispensable in the study of the Etruscan language, to an informed consideration of current anthropological theories of gift-exchange and their relevance to Archaic Etruria. These and many other revolutionary advances in Etruscan studies have been achieved by the younger generation of Italian scholars in very recent times – the first attempt at an economic history of Etruria, for example, did not appear in print until 1975. The overall result (and it is not too much to call it 'the new Etruscology') is summarized at non-specialist level for the first time in this deceptively slim volume. In a word, this is quite simply the most up-to-date account of the Etruscans that we have. That it is also brilliantly illustrated is surely not a disadvantage; there is no good reason why significant subject matter should not be presented in an aesthetically pleasing context. Finally, English readers are exceptionally fortunate in their translator. Brian Phillips has accurately rendered both the letter and the spirit of the original, and he is the only translator I know who is not too proud to seek qualified guidance in navigating the minefields inevitably encountered in even non-technical treatments of fields that are not his own. I am glad to have been of some small assistance in bringing this book to the attention of English readers.

University of Edinburgh, 1979.

David Ridgway, FSA,
Membro straniero, Istituto di Studi Etruschi ed Italici.

Introduction

The classical world has often been studied in such a way as to suggest that Etruscan civilization has its own separate cultural sphere; and this notion of separateness has in a way been intensified by a myth which has grown up about the Etruscan people, and which has itself been nurtured by popular – and sometimes ill informed – books on the subject. Consequently, if anyone now wants to make known the achievements of scientific research on the subject – and it has to be admitted that this research has been carried on within the almost impregnable ivory towers of scholarship – he has to eradicate a whole series of mistaken ideas which the more popular media continue to spread.

Where did the Etruscans come from? How can we understand their language? Questions like these have been approached in a way which has over-emphasized the 'mysteriousness' of the Etruscans, and has often added an element of science fiction to the archaeological facts. But they are questions which require an answer, and scholarly research has for some time been tackling them with the objectivity required of any scientific analysis based on facts. As far as Italy is concerned, the man responsible for initiating a scholarly approach to Etruscan studies is Massimo Pallottino. His famous book *The Etruscans*, first published in the 1940s, established the various areas of the subject worth investigation, but left it to individual scholars to pursue their own interests within those areas. Taking all the information that has become available since then – whether from literary or archaeological sources, painting or inscriptions – it has been possible to put together a completely new picture of Etruscan culture, seen as a part of the developing Mediterranean civilization of that era.

Great attention is now being paid to the different ways in which cultures change, particularly their economic and social structure, and from this point of view, the history of Etruscan civilization from the eighth to the fifth century BC is a continuous process of adaptation to external cultural influences from Greek colonies. During the eighth century the Greeks had established their own culture and founding city-states in southern Italy, at the cost of the local population. These began a process of rapid change in certain Etruscan communities, especially those on the Tyrrhenian coast, where contacts with the Greeks were frequent.

The city-state was not something static, of course, for it could have a variety of forms, and even in the Greek world it evolved to the point where it gave way to the great kingdoms of Hellenistic times. Factors such as population growth or the cultivation of different crops provided the most enterprising Greek cities with the impetus to undertake colonization. This in turn led to maritime trade and produced forms of commercial speculation and personal enrichment through the purchase and display of luxury goods as symbols of prestige. Nevertheless, the Greek city-states did have certain basic characteristics. These can be identified, for example, in the roles of the different groups which made up the populace (priests, warriors,

farmers and craftsmen), and in the relationship and rivalries between the various groups of nobles.

The influence of the Greek world was felt most strongly from the eighth to the fifth century BC, but at this same period Etruscan civilization was also related to that of Latium, for the cities of Latium – and even Rome itself until the expulsion of the last Etruscan king, Tarquinius Superbus, in 509 BC – reveal cultural affinities with Etruria, despite their dissimilar languages.

Judging from archaeological evidence and what we are told by Latin historians, the influence of Rome was strongly felt even in the larger Etruscan cities, especially those on the Tyrrhenian coast. During the reign of Servius Tullius in the first half of the sixth century BC, Rome became a firmly established city-state, and although this process had begun in the previous century, its final stages were perhaps speeded up under the influence of the Etruscan example.

From the fifth century onwards, however, Rome followed a different path. If certain specific living standards were to be obtained for the whole community, war had to become the citizens' collective duty, and since the population was made up largely of farmers, the organization of the state became jointly agricultural and military. Political power was now no longer confined to the old landed aristocracy; it was also enjoyed by other social classes, including the *plebs*. As a result, the ruling classes were infused with new blood.

In Etruria, on the other hand, the aristocratic structure of urban society remained unchanged. The ruling class continued to assert its own prerogatives, causing social struggles within many cities. In consequence, the cities became vulnerable to outside pressures and many either fell victim to Roman expansionism or were forced to accept unfavourable treaties with their aggressors.

In brief outline this book on the Etruscans begins by describing the geography of the region in which Etruscan civilization developed and shows how the action of man caused it to undergo changes. It then goes on to examine how relationships between the various social groups changed over the centuries, and how these relationships were expressed in terms of hierarchies and institutions. In order to understand social structures, however, it is vital to see how the economy worked, how labour was organized, and what forms of trade developed between the various communities and, more especially, with the Greek colonies. The last part of the book is devoted to those aspects of cultural life which reflect religious attitudes and practices and for which we have evidence in written documents.

The evidence on which this book is based is of various kinds, but since the civilization being examined is an ancient one, the bulk of it consists of the material data provided by archaeology. The interpretation of such evidence is vital if we are to outline the history of population development and manufactured goods. It is also important, however, to examine Etruscan writings and those few passages in Greek and Latin works which refer to the Etruscans, for these two kinds of evidence can be used to show, within the limits of a book intended for the general reader, what historical factors brought about the development of one particular ancient Italian civilization over a period of centuries.

Terracotta sarcophagus lid from Cerveteri (circa 480 BC; Museo Archeologico, Cerveteri), with a youth in a state of heroic semi-nudity reclining at a banquet. This physical type derives from East Greek 'aristocratic' sources.

7

Town and Country

The Transformation of the Environment

The geographical area of Italy in which Etruscan civilization developed is today divided into the three separate regions of Tuscany, Umbria and Latium, but in ancient times it had quite clearly defined natural boundaries. To the north was the basin of the river Arno, to the east and south the river Tiber, and to the west was the Tyrrhenian Sea, whose name comes from the Greek word for the Etruscans: *Týrrhenoi*. The Romans themselves were aware of the ethnic and cultural unity of the area, for, within the administrative system used by the Emperor Augustus in Italy, the boundaries of the seventh region, Etruria, followed the course of the Tiber and the Tusco-Emilian Apennines.

The physical geography of an area which stretches from the Apennines to the Tyrrhenian Sea is naturally varied. The northern part is crossed by the uplands of the Anti-Apennines. They rise up principally into the Colline Metallifere ('metal-bearing hills'), which themselves culminate in the inland spurs of Monte Amiata and Monte Cetona. The countryside is hilly almost everywhere, and any small areas of plain are mostly found along the Maremma coast. In the southern part are the mountain slopes surrounding the volcanic craters which now form lakes Bolsena, Bracciano and Vico. Here again we find a hilly countryside, rich in forests and woodlands, and crossed by a series of streams which flow into the Tiber and the Tyrrhenian Sea.

The coastline is also varied. It is high from Livorno to the mouth of the river Cecina, but then becomes lower

Rock tombs below the walls of Cerveteri (fourth century BC). The façade imitates the outside of a secular town building.

9

For the same reasons men tended to gather together in these areas, especially in river valleys such as that of the Fiora, the Val di Chiana and the Val d'Elsa. The low-lying coastal areas, especially the Maremma (comprising the whole coast from Livorno to Civitavecchia), must have had many lagoons and marshes, but at least until the third century BC, they were not malarial, for there is no solid evidence to suggest that the Maremma was as unhealthy in early times as it became later on. Roman experts in environmental theory, however, warned against siting buildings or cities near marshy places as early as the first century BC, since they realized that exhalations from stagnant water, and insects visible and invisible, were not conducive to a healthy atmosphere.

There must have been a lot of wild animals in the region. Ancient writers mention deer, goats, bears and wolves in the woods, wild boar in the scrubland and beavers in the marshland. Among the birds there must have been some kinds – especially birds of prey – which are no longer found there, for the Romans have passed down to us the Etruscan words for eagle, sparrowhawk and falcon. They themselves found these words in Etruscan books on the interpretation of the flight of birds.

Special mention must be made of the mineral deposits in the area, since the history of the Etruscans is so closely associated with their use. We do not know with any accuracy when these minerals began to be extracted, but it seems quite certain that iron ore was mined on the island of Elba and copper in the Colline Metallifere in fairly early times; and only the rich mineral deposits in the area of the Tolfa mountains can account for the flourishing culture there at the close of prehistory. On the other hand, the mines in the Val di Cecina cannot have been in use until well into historical times.

During the period of transition from prehistory to history, Etruria was inhabited by groups of men who had abandoned a nomadic life and gathered in permanent settlements in three principal geographical areas: the Tolfa mountains, the central valley of the Fiora and the land around Monte Cetona. They lived by agriculture in the widest sense of the term, not just by grazing their herds, and villages took the place of temporary or seasonal cave dwellings.

Research has revealed a considerable concentration of different kinds of settlement, some fortified with surrounding defensive walls, others open. Cemeteries have been discovered with cremation tombs in which the impasto (coarse pottery) urns are preserved in small pebble-lined shafts or tufa (a kind of porous rock) receptacles. More unusual are the stone-built tombs with funerary urns in tufa receptacles found at Crostoletto di Lamone in the Fiore valley. Within an area of about 10 square kilometres (4 square miles) around, six

and narrower as one goes farther south, except at the Piombino promontory (where the Etruscan city of Populonia was built) and around Monte Uccellina, the Argentario peninsula and the Tolfa mountains.

In ancient times the climate of the area must have been slightly different, for pollen analysis has shown that between 900 and 300 BC it was of a cold, damp, oceanic type, and surveys carried out in the Tyrrhenian Sea have confirmed that the sea level rose more than a metre between 600 BC and AD 100.

Judging from what little has survived, the natural vegetation of the region consisted of fir, beech and oak coppices close to the mountains and Mediterranean scrub towards the coast. It was chiefly in the alluvial plains and the hilly areas that man first began primitive forms of agriculture, since these were the most accessible areas and their vegetation was easier for man to cope with.

Above: View of Lake Vico. In ancient times the most densely populated of the lake areas of northern Latium was that centred on Lake Bolsena. Lake Vico is situated in the thinly populated Cimini Mountains and was one of the physical obstacles to the Roman conquest of the Etruscan hinterland.

Left: Distribution of Etruscan settlements in historical times.

settlements have been found (one surrounded by substantial walls), as well as five cremation cemeteries and one cemetery of *tumuli*. There is also a close network of settlements, bronze hoards and cremation cemeteries in the region of Allumiere, and cave deposits and upland settlements surrounded by dry-stone walls on Monte Cetona, suggesting that the area was continuously inhabited throughout the Bronze Age and into the early Iron Age as well.

Occasional scattered tombs and small cemeteries of a similar culture were discovered at Sasso di Furbara (near Cerveteri), Sticciano Scalo (near Grosseto) and in the Argentario peninsula, while in the inland part of southern Etruria, settlements of some importance have been found at Luni sul Mignone and in Lake Mezzano. These discoveries show that men tended to settle in the central and southern parts of Etruria, where natural defences were available.

These communities can be related to the general increase in population in Italy about 1000 BC, but it seems that, with certain exceptions and at different moments and in different ways, their life was disrupted by the sudden abandonment of the settlements. Although we do not know why these communities broke up, one thing is certain: the new communities began to settle where large cities would grow up in the future: along the Tyrrhenian coast (but set back a little from the sea) and near important rivers and lakes. They made use of broad tufa plateaus created through erosion by passing streams and offering natural defences. In the ninth century BC, a number of sites of this kind were occupied within a short distance of one another. Thus Veii on the right bank of the Tiber, as well as Cerveteri, Tarquinia and Vulci – all of which are only a few miles from the coast – suggest a densely inhabited area, whereas the population thins out farther north. Here we find Vetulonia and Populonia. The former is on high ground within sight of Lake Prile (now silted up and part of the plain of Grosseto) and the latter is the only settlement to be situated on a headland, in this case overlooking the island of Elba. Archaeological discoveries have also identified similar, though less substantial, inland settlements at Orvieto, overlooking the river Paglia (a tributary of the Tiber), at Chiusi, in an isolated position on a hill in the valley of the Chiana, and at Volterra, on raised ground overlooking the Cecina. The choice of site for these early settlements seems to have been dictated by certain specific factors, such as the availability of large areas for cultivation, easy communications by sea or river, and the presence of minerals (in the Tolfa mountains, the Colline Metallifere near Grosseto, and the Montecatini-Val di Cecina area near Volterra).

It is thus possible to identify in Etruria certain settlements which, at the end of the ninth century, could be

Above: The rock of Orvieto on which stood the Etruscan city of Volsinii (Velsna). Classical writers make particular mention of its strategic position and impregnability.

Right: Hut urn from Vetulonia (late ninth to early eighth century BC; Museo Archeologico, Florence). This symbolic representation of a contemporary dwelling was used for burying the ashes of a cremated woman.

Below: Distribution of villages and cemeteries in the territory of Veii, showing how people were grouped in an Iron Age settlement, before the city of Veii grew up on the same plateau.

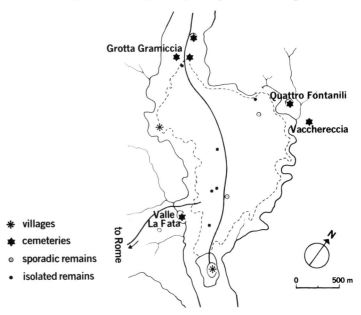

Grotta Gramiccia

Quattro Fontanili

Vacchereccia

Valle La Fata

to Rome

✳ villages
✦ cemeteries
◦ sporadic remains
• isolated remains

N

0   500 m

defined as pre-urban. The fact that their cemeteries were situated at quite separate spots around the tufa plateaus provides evidence about the internal arrangement of the settlements, because it suggests that, while groups of several hundred families lived in the same area, they occupied separate villages of huts on the edges of the plateau and used the substantial areas left free between their villages for tilling the land and raising animals. There is no doubt, too, that even in the sixth and fifth centuries BC, when cities had developed and were inhabited by thousands of people, certain areas of the tufa plateaus must still have been reserved for farming. Some idea of how this worked can be obtained by measuring the area of walled cities. Inland cities were the smallest. Chiusi barely covered 26 hectares (64 acres) and Volsinii (Orvieto) about 40 hectares (100 acres) – a sure sign that farming must have been carried on in the plains outside the cities themselves. Cerveteri,

Tarquinia and Vulci covered respectively 120, 150 and 180 hectares (300, 370 and 445 acres), while the largest cities, in terms of area, were Veii with 243 hectares (600 acres) and Volterra, whose fourth-century walls enclose as much as 260 hectares (about 640 acres). This shows that some farming could, if necessary, be carried on within the confines of the city itself.

Contacts with Greek settlers in the closing decades of the eighth century BC brought a series of social and economic changes in coastal communities and so affected population patterns. Places which had been inhabited in proto-historic times were reoccupied, and new sites for settlements were chosen, for example in the valleys of the Albegna and the Fiora, to provide river communications with coastal communities. A substantial population gathered at Tuscania on the river Marta, which flows out of Lake Bolsena, and a close network of small settlements grew up in the Fosso

Biedano area, between the Tolfa mountains and the impenetrable Selva Ciminia. Unfortunately, few excavations have been carried out in the settlements themselves, so that it is impossible to establish their relative importance. Their position, however, clearly shows that defence was a basic factor in choice of site, for they are situated on plateaus created by river erosion which are either completely isolated or connected to the surrounding area only by a narrow neck of land. The kind of site chosen suggests small settlements with natural defences (similar to the Roman *oppida*), quite unlike the much smaller, scattered settlements organized in villages.

Archaeological evidence suggests that these minor towns must, in effect, have been dependencies of the big coastal settlements, for luxury consumer goods arrived there directly from the craftsmen who had been setting themselves up in the coastal cities, each of which was by now virtually a metropolis. At Veii, Cerveteri, Tarquinia and Vulci the process of urbanization seems to have accelerated during the seventh century BC, and was complete by its closing decades. By then the normal site for a city was a large tufa plateau, with a distinct citadel where the city's gods were worshipped (such as that at Veii) and a walled urban area (for example at Roselle). At the period of its full development, the city became the centre for every kind of craft and trading activity, and Greek merchants were welcome – in fact classical writers tell us that a few of them settled there permanently.

At this stage, two particular cities became pre-eminent in southern Etruria. One was Caere (Cerveteri), with its fairly extensive hinterland, including secondary towns in the Viterbo area (Luni, S. Giovenale, Blera and Norchia), to which lines of communication such as the river Mignone provided access. The other was Vulci, with its secondary towns not only on the banks of the

Right: Painted impasto cinerary urn from Cerveteri (650–630 BC; Museo Archeologico, Cerveteri). Its external appearance is that of a building with acroteria *on the ridge-beam of its gabled roof.*

Left, above: The reddish tufa-rock formation on whose plateau stood the city of Caere (Cerveteri).

Left, below: The village of Pitigliano as it is today, with houses built on rock foundations. This recalls the physical appearance of a medium-sized settlement in the Etruscan hinterland.

river Fiora (Castro, Poggio Buco and Sovana) but also along the coast as far as Orbetello, where a port community grew up, and along the river Albegna from Marsiliana and Magliano to Saturnia.

The situation in the Grosseto area, around Lake Prile, was different. Because of its concern to exploit mineral deposits, Vetulonia expanded its territory in a different way: chiefly along a line leading into the Colline Metallifere as far as Lake Accesa. The community which settled on the Roselle plateau in the seventh century BC had the river Ombrone (then navigable) as a means of communication with areas farther inland, and its principal activity was probably farming.

It has already been mentioned that the Monte Cetona area was of considerable cultural influence in protohistoric times, and in fact two rivers rise in this range of mountains: the Paglia on the southern side and the Orcia to the north. In historical times the population was

scattered in small upland settlements. Some were on the southern slopes (Cancelli and S. Casciano ai Bagni) and others on the northern slopes towards Sarteano, and at Chianciano and Chiusi beyond the river Astrone.

None of these settlements, however, was similar in type to southern Etrurian towns, at any rate during the seventh and the first half of the sixth century. The population seems to have been scattered in small village units, rather like the inland part of northern Etruria as well as the Val di Chiana and the Val d'Elsa. The settlements most likely to attract immigrants were those situated on the principal lines of communication. Orvieto is a good example, for it is situated on a rocky height overlooking the confluence of the Paglia and the Tiber; and, as classical writers tell us, the Tiber attracted a great deal of traffic, since it was navigable for a nine days' journey upstream from the mouth.

The Growth of Cities

How did these settlements become cities? In trying to answer this question, we must avoid paying too much attention to the physical creation of the city, because that was simply a result of preceding social and economic changes. One theory as to how cities came into being is supplied by ancient philosophy. Groups of men came down from the mountains and settled in the country-side below, erecting wooden fences as a protection against wild animals and building a large communal dwelling. Settlements created in this way subsequently expanded by absorbing their neighbours, but each remained loyal to its original community by tradition and obedience, until a lawgiver came on the scene and established rules to govern the relationships between groups, in the form of a constitution which provided guarantees to all. This is the Platonic view of the problem

Right: The defensive walls of the town of Roselle, near Grosseto. (Their circuit of 3270 metres surrounded the whole urban area.) Although subsequently rebuilt, they were originally set up in the mid-sixth century BC, at a time when city life was coming into its own.

Left: Tomba della Capanna, Cerveteri. One of the earliest chamber tombs (first half of the seventh century BC). The application to tombs of the forms of dwellings leads here to the representation of a hut interior.

(*Laws* III, 680–1). Here the institutional aspect of the city is stressed; but that, too, is the result of changes in social and economic relationships. Let us now look at the example of Rome shortly before the mid–sixth century BC. The king of Rome at the time was Servius Tullius, a man of Etruscan origin who had come to power in mysterious circumstances – perhaps by means of a personal coup. The reforms he carried out make it clear that there were definite social tensions underlying his political programme. The population was divided into classes by wealth and landed property rather than birth, and sanctuaries were set up outside the city walls as market places for trade with other communities. This shows that economic forces were at work involving social classes other than the old landed aristocracy. In Rome, the area near the Forum Boarium became the 'commercial quarter', and it was here that Servius

Tullius built a temple to Fortune, the divinity directly responsible for the safety of the city. In the case of the Etruscans, on the other hand, it was coastal settlements with port facilities which were developed, for they were places for trading with the Greeks and Phoenicians, as one can tell by their names. Thus the ports for Cerveteri were Pyrgi (from the Greek *pýrgoi* meaning 'towers') and Punicum (an obvious reference to the Carthaginians), and the port for Vulci was Rege (from the Greek *régai* meaning 'rocky places'). Furthermore, recent excavations at Gravisca, the port for Tarquinia, show that Greek merchants were to be found there and were busy establishing their sanctuaries along the coast from about 580 to 480 BC.

Unfortunately, too few systematic investigations have been carried out to tell us much about the physical appearance of Etruscan cities at this period. Some recent excavations in minor settlements in the Viterbo area which were destroyed about the end of the sixth century, make it clear that there was no urban planning there at that time; and the same is true of the limited urban areas of Veii and Roselle explored so far. Houses consisted of a small number of rooms arranged in a row, sometimes with a porch at the front. Their walls might be made of stone blocks or, more frequently, of unbaked bricks or wood and compressed clay. Compared with these rough and ready buildings, much more care was taken with the areas set aside for religious purposes, and with kings' 'palaces'. During the sixth century, in fact, a particular type of monumental architecture was developed for constructing the latter kind of building. It seems certain, therefore, that the regular plan found at Marzabotto in Emilia cannot be typical of Etruscan cities. Marzabotto came into being at the beginning of the fifth century BC, with all the special characteristics of a city founded by colonists in the wake of a series of changes in the population of the whole of inland Etruria. That cities finally emerged as magnets for the population of a given area can be deduced not only from the abandonment of the inhabited parts of the countryside near Viterbo and the valleys of the Fiora and the Albegna at the end of the sixth century, but also from the desertion of villages in the Val di Chiana in favour of Chiusi, and from the tendency for people to settle in Arezzo and Volterra. The forced evacuation of minor towns is a sign that the chief cities were becoming aware of their status as independent political units with control over the surrounding territory, and the regional states which were thus formed had a common ethnic basis which allowed them to form a confederation of the 'twelve peoples of Etruria', which met once a year at the Voltumna sanctuary near Volsinii (Orvieto) to elect a military commander-in-chief.

The cemetery at Orvieto in fact provides us with a detailed example, from the closing decades of the

The Tuscan countryside near Grosseto. The relationship between town and country in Etruria depends historically on the area concerned. Generally speaking, the period of urban development brought with it a considerable concentration of population inside cities and depopulation of the countryside, where the remaining inhabitants were in small settlements or isolated dwellings. During the second century BC, when agriculture was the chief productive occupation, the countryside of Umbria and the interior of Tuscany became reinhabited with scattered settlements and farming estates.

sixth century, of how urban planning could work, for the arrangement of the family tombs in 'streets', with regular frontages and similar internal structure must be the result of a specific political decision, possibly emanating from the state authority itself. Recent excavations in the cemetery at Cerveteri also bear witness to a similar kind of political control at the same period. In this case, uniformity was imposed on the preceding disordered conglomeration of tombs, where the differing wealth of the various families was partly reflected in the different physical bulk of the tombs.

The imposition of this kind of uniformity is the result of the application to cemeteries of a new concept of the 'functional' organization of cities; but it does not imply that there was a parallel uniformity of wealth. Each tomb is strictly reserved for a family of freemen, and the head of the family, who is the titular owner of the tomb, accepts the 'external' standardization of the cemetery, whatever the wealth of his own family, for that is re-

flected in the quantity and nature of the tomb furnishings.

In making a comparison between the arrangement of these cemeteries and that of the town of Marzabotto, it must be remembered that the town concerned was a commercial and industrial one, founded at the beginning of the fifth century. It was situated at the foot of the Apennines near the river Reno, which flows past Bologna (Etruscan 'Felsina') and into the Adriatic Sea. Its regular plan, such as occurs in other Etruscan cities founded by colonists at the same period (Capua, for example), may be the result of a specifically Etruscan ritual for dividing up land (we know quite a lot about such rituals – see page 107), in which the divisions of the heavens used in the art of divination are applied to the earth. It is quite possible, however, that the influence of rational Greek town planning is also at work here, for it was being codified at this time, and may be reflected in the functional arrangement of the various areas at Marzabotto. Thus the sanctuaries are on the so-called 'acropolis' outside the town to the west; the cemeteries are to the north and east; and, within the city, the 'public' area is distinct from the residential quarters. The way individual blocks of houses are arranged is particularly significant. All are the same length, about 165 metres (540 feet), with the house fronts facing the streets. These have pavements along their sides and are provided with drains. The houses themselves are rectangular, and their individual rooms are arranged round a central courtyard. Judging from tomb furnishings, there must have been a fairly even distribution of wealth amongst the inhabitants, and we can conclude that they were socially and economically homogeneous; this is reflected in the uniform arrangement of their houses.

The case of Spina on the Po delta – another city founded by colonists – seems to be similar. The town plan is again arranged along straight axes. The houses were made of light materials anchored into the sandy soil and reinforced round the outside with rows of piles. Floors were laid on beds of clay. In addition to the streets, there were also canals which served to link the town itself and the river. In ancient times the Etruscans were famous for their skill in hydraulics, and Spina seems to have been the result of a vast piece of land reclamation, intended to cope with a series of water problems in the area. According to Pliny the Elder (*Natural History*, III, 16), the Etruscans were responsible for all the land reclamation carried out at the mouth of the river Po, using canals and offtakes to steer the inconveniently fast-flowing river waters towards the marshes of Adria.

The growth of large cities, described above, entered a period of crisis in the fifth century. During the first thirty years of the century, there were a number of major wars between the Greeks and their 'barbarian' enemies (the Persians in the east and the Carthaginians in the west). The Etruscans were also involved and were defeated by the forces of Syracuse in a naval battle off Cumae in 474 BC. Without the Etruscans in control of the sea routes, the Greeks began to abandon the coast of Etruria and seek new trading stations along the Adriatic, although they continued to obtain supplies of minerals from Populonia. But while Etruscan coastal cities went into decline for a century, inland cities enjoyed considerable prosperity. At the beginning of the fourth century, Chiusi had more territory than its inhabitants could cultivate. Although sparsely populated, the countryside was rich in vineyards and olive trees as well as grain, and was so extensive that when the Gauls came down into Italy and made their way towards Rome, some of it could be handed over to them (Dionysius of Halicarnassus, *Roman Antiquities*, XIII, 16).

The landed nobles who lived in the cities close to the Tiber valley fared even better, because they could exploit the fertile soil and the good communications offered by the Tiber, which was not only navigable but could be used for floating timber down from the forests. During the fifth century, the whole territory of Veii became scattered with irrigation and water conservation schemes, all designed to improve agriculture, using an abundance of *cuniculi* (drainage channels).

By the mid-fourth century when the Etruscan states were faced with Roman expansionism, their territory was reorganized in the sense that the population had been redistributed. The abandoned settlements in the Fiora valley took on a new lease of life; the old fortified settlements in the Viterbo area (now under the rule of Tarquinia) were reoccupied; and villages reappeared around Lake Bolsena in the territory of Volsinii.

Rome took military action against those Etruscan states which were their immediate neighbours or were at least in a strategically favourable position. Their organization was good, and they caught the Etruscans quite unprepared. While those Etruscan cities belonging to the 'league' did have annual assemblies, these had no particular political significance, partly because the 'league' was basically a religious institution and partly because of the independent policies of the different states. Once the Romans had destroyed Veii in 396 BC – without the other Etruscan cities coming to its aid – they seem to have been chiefly concerned with expansion along the Tiber valley and the Tyrrhenian coast. At the end of the fourth century and during the early decades of the third, the wars between Romans and Etruscans intensified and led in some cases to the final destruction of Etruscan cities (Volsinii in 264 BC and Falerii in 248 BC), and in others to the acceptance of very unfavourable treaties of alliance.

Tarquinia was reduced to seeking a forty-year truce after decades of strife and then, at the beginning of the third century, Caere and Vulci lost a large part of their territory, the land concerned becoming state-owned Roman property. The *fasti* show that Roman consuls had as many as seven victories over the Etruscans between 311 and 281 BC, and two more were recorded in 280: one over Volsinii and another over Vulci.

In the view of Greek and Roman writers, the Etruscan urban ruling class was now definitely in decline. Hence the severe social unrest at Arezzo in the fourth century and at Volsinii in the first half of the third century showed that the aims of the slaves' revolts was to obtain rights which Rome had long since granted to the *plebs*. If we read between the lines of these ancient accounts, with their moralizing attitudes, we can see that the ruling class was in fact defending itself on the basis of its ancient rights, but could not really cope with the social pressures being brought to bear upon it. In the case of Volsinii, the effect of an attempt to solve the internal crisis by means of the mass emancipation of the slaves was to precipitate events. The state seems to have had no option but to call in the Romans to assist in a sort of police operation, even though it was thus forced to come to terms with the best organized city in Latium.

The Roman state was so highly organized on a military and agricultural basis that in 273 BC it was able to found a colony on the coast at Cosa, right inside the territory of Vulci, without any prior negotiation with the Etruscans. Indeed, in the first half of the third century, colonies were founded in a number of places along the coastal territory of Caere, including the Etruscan ports, and the rich inland territory of Vulci was reduced to the status of a Roman prefecture.

At the time when the large Etruscan cities were being destroyed or obliged to accept alliances with Rome,

Above: The cemetery at Cerveteri. Towards the end of the sixth century BC, *its tombs were organized in a functional way. Hence in this area of the cemetery, known as the Via dei Monti della Tolfa, tombs built to a standard plan are found alongside Archaic tumuli.*

Preceding pages: Interior of the Tomba degli Scudi e delle Sedie at Cerveteri (circa mid–sixth century BC*). It reproduces the* atrium *of an 'aristocratic' house with chairs and shields hanging on the wall.*

the inland cities by contrast seem to have taken on a new lease of life, and even to have gained political independence. If we look at Sovana in the territory of Vulci, or Tuscania, Norchia and Blera in the territory of Tarquinia, or Bomarzo and Ferento in the southern part of the territory of Volsinii, we find that, although situated on Roman consular roads (the Via Clodia and the Via Cassia), they were now reviving earlier urban traditions. There is evidence of this in their rock cemeteries, where the tomb fronts are hewn out of the tufa rock, as though to underline the fact that this was a specifically 'urban' architecture.

In the Roman colonies, land had originally been distributed among individual farmers, many of whom were ex-soldiers. But during the second century, rural organization began to disintegrate; the colonies were becoming depopulated and the countryside was being concentrated in the hands of a few skilful landowners who used slave labour to run new large farm units on the *latifundium* system. As he travelled along the Via Aurelia in 135 BC, Tiberius Gracchus observed that the countryside seemed to have been abandoned by the old Roman farmers and was now cultivated by foreign slaves.

In the inland part of northern Etruria the situation was different. Some of the most important cities, such as Volterra and Arezzo, maintained their pre-eminent position. Only at Perugia and Chiusi was there a substantial change in the distribution of the population, and it may be that this was brought about by yet another slave revolt in 196 BC. By the mid-second century the whole of the Val di Chiana was occupied by scattered settlements with the farms run by freed slaves or freemen labourers; and large suburban areas grew up a short distance from the centre of Perugia. Crops suitable for commercial speculation – especially the olive and the grape – were developed, partly for trade with Rome; and the once rich but sparsely populated countryside was now tilled by plebeians who were at last gaining certain guaranteed rights, including, perhaps, the right to own land. In other words, farming was now organized in a new way, which was to persist until Rome decided on a different distribution of land in 90 BC. That meant the end for this part of Etruria, and by AD 15 it already showed alarming signs of becoming marshland.

Right: Plan of Marzabotto, a late sixth-century BC Etruscan 'colony'. The regular urban layout was begun in the first half of the fifth century BC. The various areas of the city are not arranged according to their function, for shops and ateliers seem to have been established along the most heavily used streets.

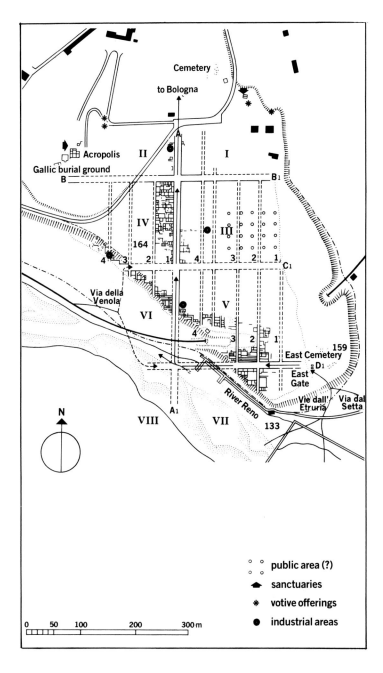

The Family and Social Organization

The Development of the Family

From its earliest beginnings, Etruscan society seems to have been based on the traditional family. The well tombs in the Villanovan urn-fields were, it is true, similar to one another, and each was made for one person; and while the tomb furnishings tell us the sex of the dead person, they do not reveal anything of his relationship to the other dead. Nevertheless, there are a few cemeteries, such as the one at Sorbo near Cerveteri, where adjacent trench or well tombs seem to belong to family groups.

Iron Age villagers were not nomadic; they lived by farming. Each village housed a number of families in huts of similar type. They were oval or circular in plan, with floors hewn out of the rock or else of clay, and were constructed of the same light materials – wooden poles, branches and mud – that we find represented in funerary urns of the period.

It may be that this basic social structure somehow derives from the patriarchal family, as in the case of the Romans. The egalitarian appearance of both tombs and houses might suggest an ethnic group organized in a large undivided family (later split up into nuclear families), each economically self-sufficient and with a *pater familias* who represented, as it were, a common ancestor and founder of the race. In the second half of the seventh century, however, we find votive offerings in small rural sanctuaries in northern Etruria, which provide evidence of families based on husband and wife. There are bronze figures not only of individual

Gravestone from Chiusi (500–480 BC; Museo Baracco, Rome). Two seated women are shown looking at mantles held up by other women. The scene probably represents preparations for a ceremony.

men, dressed only in loincloths and holding lances, but also of veiled women and animals, mostly cattle. The fact that these three kinds of small bronze figure appear together suggests that rural society had a family basis and was concerned with farming and warfare. There is also later archaeological evidence to suggest that Etruscan family relationships were built round the position of the father.

During the seventh century, when large Etruscan cities were coming into being, their system of personal names took the form of the same two basic elements used in western society today: an individual name and a family name. As happens in the Latin system, so in Etruscan the family name is formed by adding a suffix to a personal name. Thus, for example, we find in Latin a personal name *Marcus* and a family name *Marcius*, and there are corresponding forms *Marce* and *Marcena* in Etruscan. In this case, then, the ancestral founder of the family is a 'Mark', and all those who think of themselves as his descendants add to their personal name a family name. It is not until the end of the sixth century that one begins to find funerary inscriptions – and such inscriptions have, after all, a semi-official status – in which a third element is added to the names of persons to indicate paternal authority.

As urban communities developed, so did the use of chamber tombs, in which all funerary inscriptions referring to women show that when a woman married she became part of her husband's family, for it was in their tomb that women were buried. In the cemetery at Orvieto, mentioned earlier, there are late sixth-century inscriptions which make it quite clear that the owner of the tomb concerned, and hence of the family property generally, was a man. Out of more than one hundred tombs, only five per cent have an inscription designating a woman as an owner of property. This kind of evidence led scholars some time ago to reject the myth that Etruscan society was a matriarchy.

While it was exceptional for a woman to own land, the same was not true of everyday objects. From the seventh century onwards, there are inscriptions indicating that women did own such things. Evidently the social class of those who could read and write contained women as well as men. Etruscan women certainly enjoyed more freedom than their Greek and Roman counterparts. Inscriptions show that, like men, they had personal and family names, whereas Roman women were identified only by a family name – perhaps as a result of a name taboo which concealed the fact that a woman was subject first to the control of her father and then of her husband. There are sixth-century family tombs at Cerveteri whose tufa-rock interiors are like the rooms of a house, and the funerary beds of the women are identified by a triangular pediment which is an obvious allusion to the roof of a house. Although the

freedom enjoyed by Etruscan women was usually limited to the home, it could also extend to public activities such as watching games, as one can see from sixth-century paintings. This scandalized Greek and Roman writers. The Greeks and Romans lived in a society where women were responsible for running homes, and where it was inconceivable that wives should be present at men's banquets. The very fact that there were private or public courtesans at Greek banquets, for example, shows that in Greece, and in Rome too, erotic activities were kept outside the family.

The degree of freedom which women enjoyed depended on their social class. Thus classical writers stress, for example, the important part played by Tanaquil, wife of Tarquinius Priscus, in Servius Tullius's succession to the throne of Rome. In the large fourth-century tombs of the nobility in southern Etruria there

Left: Painted black-figure krater *from Cerveteri (circa 675–650* BC; *Museo Archeologico, Cerveteri). This detail shows a married couple – the basic unit of Etruscan society – with the woman taking the man by the arm.*

Right: Terracotta frieze plaque from the 'palace' of Murlo (circa mid-sixth century BC; *Palazzo Comunale, Siena). A married couple (presumably 'dynasts') are shown in a carriage, taking part in a procession. They are protected by an umbrella, which may be a symbol of their royal status.*

are inscriptions in which the nobles make much of their ancestry, and the names of the dead include a form to indicate the mother of the dead person, placed after that used to indicate the father. The fact that the family ramifications of the nobility were so extensive suggests, moreover, that marriage was part of a system of group relationships involving a kind of inbreeding amongst the landed aristocracy. The many second-century inscriptions on funerary urns in the territory of Chiusi and Perugia show that the use of name forms to indicate a person's mother and father had spread beyond the nobility, but as a rule, a woman's husband's name was placed after her own full name.

The typical family was monogamous, and this had its effect on the form and organization of the home. At the time when urban culture was at its most highly developed, the design of houses and tombs is parallel. As in earlier times, areas were set aside for cemeteries outside the city, and the fact that they contained tombs in the form of chambers is itself an indication of the fully urban nature of society. Furthermore, the city dwellers lived in houses which tended to conform to an average standard, though they might vary in accordance with the needs of the family concerned. The main room had a fireplace in the middle or to one side – in which case a chimney was provided. A second room communicated with the first and was probably used as a bedroom. There might be other rooms of secondary importance as well, but the central room remained what one might call the 'public' room. The house might have a portico in front of the entrance, and while ovens and wells were outside, grain stores were inside, in specially dug compartments. Houses such as these are found at Veii and Acquarossa in the fourth century. They belong, that is to say, to cities where the building of houses went on without a preconceived plan. It is likely that where

sixth-century houses have a more elaborate plan, with a vestibule and three rooms arranged in a row at the back – which also occurs in tombs in the territory of Cerveteri – they are of the most aristocratic type, for this was the form used in three-chamber temples.

At Marzabotto, on the other hand, individual houses, like the city itself, seem to be the result of planning. There are blocks of slightly different sizes, each containing a number of houses, and each house stretches the full depth of the block. The arrangement of the rooms in each house is not uniform, but the houses are designed lengthwise, with an entrance corridor leading into a square central room, sometimes with a well in it. Other strictly rectangular rooms are arranged round it, along the lines of the layout of the whole city. This type of house arrangement seems to have become popular later on. In the Hellenistic quarter at Roselle, for example, the rooms in ordinary houses are arranged round courtyards with wells, while in the particular areas of the city set aside for upper-class houses, one finds that their rooms are arranged round arcaded courtyards.

Social Hierarchies

So far in this chapter, the known facts have been used to outline the way the Etruscan family was structured, and there is no doubt that this system persisted until the decline of Etruscan civilization, although some large Hellenistic tombs suggest that at a late stage the upper classes were organized in groups larger than the family.

We have also identified basic social and economic units from the Iron Age onwards, and we have used different kinds of evidence to establish their existence at different periods, sometimes indicating the particular social levels involved. It is now necessary to examine how Etruscan social and economic history developed alongside changes in the population.

Within Iron Age villages, with their numerous families, class differences came into being at an early stage, as a result of contacts with the Phoenicians and Greeks. As has already been explained, the direction and and extent of population distribution at the beginning of the seventh century was largely controlled by certain southern cities. This is where different social classes first appear, and they suggest that the organization of the community was breaking up. Family tombs with several burials may contain quantities of luxury goods which had been acquired through maritime trade with Greece and other eastern countries. This is evidence of the emergence of an aristocracy which was establishing its position as a result of the personal acquisition of wealth from Greek colonies – obtained by a variety of means stretching from legitimate bartering to downright piracy.

The patriarchal characteristics of the head of a family were changing, in the sense that he was now in control not only of the means of production and cultural expression (writing, for example, which had been introduced by the Euboean Greeks and modified to suit Etruscan requirements at the beginning of the seventh century), but also of certain prestige objects such as his weapons, chariot and seat of authority, which indicated his rank even in the tomb. At the same time members of society seemed to gather round a particular 'leader', and their subordination to him was based on his position not only as family head but also as one in control of patronage. In other words, individuals or groups of people acknowledge the authority of a 'leader' for a variety of different reasons. They enjoy his protection, but at the same time owe him certain specific kinds of respect or service, ranging from service in his private army (vital at a time when there was a great deal of warfare or skirmishing between rival groups) to tilling his fields.

How long this new aristocracy-based structure lasted depended on when and how urban society as such became established. The small settlement at Murlo, near Siena, provides an example of a society controlled by individual aristocrats who still held the reins of religious and political power in the mid-sixth century. The settlement in question consists of an architectural complex which one might describe as the ruler's 'palace', and he is in fact represented, together with the insignia of his office, on decorative revetment plaques. He is seated, and holds in his hand the *lituus* as a symbol of his religious authority. He is served by a standing slave, who bears his weapons (a sword and lance), and behind him is his wife. She, too, is seated on a sumptuous throne, and is served by a girl who stands

with a fan and a pail in her hands. Then come the seated figures of two women and a man, who may be their children. The man has a two-edged axe as a symbol of political authority. This 'palace' can be related to some imposing chamber tombs of the first half of the sixth century in isolated positions in the countryside of inland northern Etruria: at Castellina in Chianti, Cortona, Quinto Fiorentino, and in the territory of Volterra. It appears that the accumulation of prestige and luxury goods started much later inland than in coastal settlements.

At this period, the authority of the 'leader' evolves into that of a king, about whom Greek and Roman writers provide occasional pieces of information. 'In Etruscan, kings are called *lucumones*.' Their insignia were, we are told, 'a gold crown, an ivory throne, a sceptre surmounted by an eagle, a purple tunic threaded with gold, and a cloak, also of purple, with embroidered

This series of illustrations shows the relationship between sacred and secular building. A, B and C below are plans of typical sixth-century buildings, while D, E and F show typical arrangements of the chambers in tombs at Cerveteri. An example of type F is the Tomba degli Scudi e delle Sedie (see pp. 22–23), which imitates the arrangement of an 'aristocratic' house. A similar layout is found in the Temple of Jupiter Capitolinus (below right), which was built by the Etruscan kings of Rome and inaugurated in 507 BC. The latter building increases the relative size of the colonnaded space outside the doors, with the temple's three cellae devoted to the cult of the triad (Jupiter, Juno and Minerva). The Tomba G. Moretti at Cerveteri dates to the end of the sixth century BC. Its atrium (above right) is reminiscent of the structural arrangement of the space outside the doors of a temple: note the roof beams, the columns (with their Doric capitals and moulded bases), and the doorways into the cellae in the rear wall (on the left in the photograph).

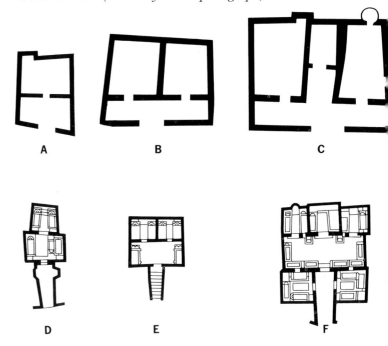

A   B   C

D   E   F

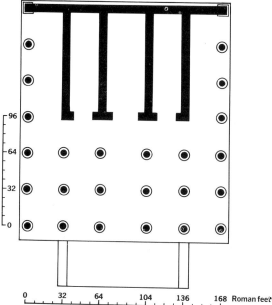

decoration'. It was 'an Etruscan custom for the king to be preceded by a lictor, who carried an axe held together by a bundle of rods'. Thus the symbols of royal power apparently came to Rome from Etruria and were mostly related to political authority (crown, throne, sceptre and *fasces*).

In southern Etruria, the process of social differentiation seems to go a stage further in the closing decades of the seventh century. Wealth is more evenly distributed in tombs, and the tombs themselves are more alike. In other words, although the aristocratic system persists, a substantial urban class of craftsmen and merchants, including foreigners, is coming into being. Advances in manufactures, especially pottery and bronzework, together with commercial expansion by sea as well as land, have brought into existence a middle class, separate from the aristocracy. This new social class was to constitute the basis of urban population, and Servius

Tullius, the Etruscan king of Rome from 578 to 535 BC (a much less legendary figure than is often supposed), was to classify its members according to their wealth and hence their ability to serve the state in a military capacity.

The figure of the 'tyrant-liberator', who overthrows the system controlled by the old landed aristocracy and instils new vigour into the state, is one which also appears in the large urban communities of southern Etruria. A person of this kind is in fact named in the late sixth-century dedicatory inscriptions in Phoenician and Etruscan, found on gold plaques in the sanctuary at Pyrgi, one of the ports for Caere. Here is part of what he has to say in the Phoenician text:

> This is the sacred place that *Thefarie Velianas*, ruler of Caere, has built and offered to the lady Astarte in the month of the sun sacrifice, as a gift in the sanctuary. I (*Thefarie Velianas*) have built

it because Astarte requested it of me in the third year of my reign, in the month of *krr*, on the day of the burial of the goddess.

The corresponding inscription in Etruscan is much less easy to understand, but supplies the same information: *Thefarie Velianas* has dedicated a votive chapel and a statue to *Uni* (the most important of the Etruscan goddesses and the equivalent of the Phoenician goddess Astarte). The reasons for this dedication in both texts may have something to do with the public office held by *Thefarie Velianas*. He seems to have been a magistrate of Cerveteri whose tenure of office was not annual (the Etruscan term for this is *zilac*), and who enjoyed the protection of a goddess. In accordance with a custom of eastern origin – but of vital importance to Greek tyrants at this period – he had a charismatic power which emanated from the goddess. This is the religious connotation which allowed a tyrant to claim

Left: View of the remaining foundations of houses at Marzabotto. In a planned city like this, dwellings were intended for individual families, and were arranged round an internal courtyard. Since one of the purposes of the city was to trade with people who were 'passing through', rooms facing onto the street were used as 'shops'.

Below: Impasto helmet from an Iron Age cremation tomb at Tarquinia (Museo Archeologico, Florence). It was used as the cover of a burial urn, thereby indicating the prestige, or rather social rank, of the dead person.

special powers for himself, though with the consent of social groups who were not involved in politics because they had no political rights.

The position of Servius Tullius in Rome also throws some light on Etruria. He gained the throne of Rome by arbitrarily claiming a place in the dynastic line of the Tarquins. His Etruscan name, *Macstrna*, can be related to the Latin *magister* ('leader' or 'guide') – a word whose etymology suggests rather a special military leader. Latin sources say that 'he had granted liberty to the citizens'. The reforms of Servius Tullius were primarily concerned with the Roman army, but they clearly involved considerable innovations of a more general kind. All those who were resident in the city and had sufficient means (calculated primarily on land possession), were required to serve in the state army and pay taxes if required. The non-property-owning proletariat, however, was exempted from military service. The property-owning class was subdivided into five groups, according to their wealth, and each of these was itself subdivided into centuries. There were 170 centuries altogether, 98 of which consisted of the very wealthy and knights, and it was they who took part in the assemblies arranged for electing the most important magistrates and passing laws. Military conscription was organized territorially, through a series of urban and rural districts, which took into account the latest form of the city: now surrounded by walls and no longer divided into three, as had traditionally been the case.

It may be that a similar arrangement operated in Etruria, for there is a passage in Festus in which he provides a summary of the Etruscan 'ritual books' and says that they deal with 'the rites used in founding a city, how altars and temples are consecrated, the inviolability attributed to city walls, how tribes, centuries and curias are organized, how armies are raised and organized, and similar matters concerning wartime and peacetime arrangements'.

It was in these books, then, that Etruscan law was set down. On the one hand the city area was sacred because the division of land was sacred (this will be examined in greater detail in the chapter on Etruscan religious life), and on the other administrative law was based on the organization of the army, as in the case of the reforms of Servius Tullius. As in Rome, military conscription was based on the individual's ability to supply himself with a complete suit of armour, including helmet, breastplate, greaves, shield, lance and spear. Barely fifty years earlier, this Greek type of armour had been the prerogative of the 'chiefs' and their entourage, but it was now in much more widespread use, for heavily armed foot-soldiers played a major role in contemporary warfare.

The city-like, planned layout of the cemeteries at

Cerveteri and Orvieto are evidence that city dwellers belonged to a new social class. The age of the large monumental *tumulus* has gone, and so has that of the aristocratic 'chief'. The city is a sacred area inhabited by the citizens and physically separated from the rest of its territory by its walls. Foreigners, especially merchants, are granted areas outside the city for their religious practices and business activities. At one time trade had been a matter of individual initiative, but now it became subject to definite rules and regulations, which may have been laid down by the city authorities.

According to Roman writers, Servius Tullius was also responsible for establishing 'units of measurement and weight', and was 'the first to mark bronze with a seal'. In other words, he used the seal of state authority to guarantee the worth of bronze in its use for trading purposes. There were indeed bronze ingots of varying weights in circulation in Etruria and Latium in the

second half of the sixth century with a dead twig sign impressed on them. They have been found principally in areas colonized by the Etruscans (the coast of Campania and central and western Emilia), but also as far afield as Sicily (Gela) and Croatia. So the state authority was now guaranteeing bronze which already had a specific value for trading purposes, even though in a rough and ready form. Struck coins, on the other hand, must have been limited in their use to small-scale trading. They were always made of precious metals such as gold and silver and appear only sporadically where trade was carried on at its most vigorous, for example at Populonia and Vulci. They were probably issued by individuals for special purposes, because they do not reappear until much later.

In the second half of the sixth century, then, life centred on the cities, for it was here that the state authority was situated and trading went on. This was

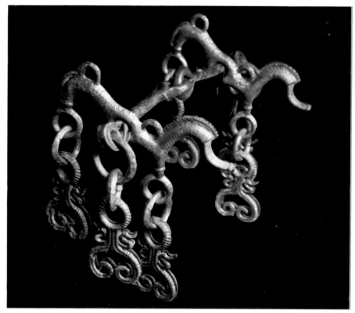

Left: Bronze funerary urn showing a cult ceremony taking place around a totem. From Bisenzio (end of the eighth century BC; *Museo di Villa Giulia, Rome). A prisoner is chained to the totem. The various warriors and the peasant involved in the ceremony are indicative of social roles in late Iron Age society.*

Right: Bronze horse bit (Museo di Villa Giulia, Rome). Presumably from a tomb dating to the second half of the eighth century BC. *It serves to indicate the dead man's place in the social and military hierarchy.*

Below: Terracotta acroterion *from the 'palace' of Murlo (circa 550* BC; *Palazzo Comunale, Siena). This imposing seated figure was intended to hold the insignia of command in his hands. Statues like this one were set up in a row along the top of the roof and were probably intended to represent ancestors.*

the time when the Etruscan city modelled itself on the Greek city-state (*polis*), adopting not only the outward aspects of its religious ideology (the physical appearance of the Etruscan gods, for example, now imitated that of Greek religious images), but also its secular organization, particularly that of the ruling classes.

This accounts for the changes in population distribution mentioned earlier. Minor towns, which were still run on the old aristocratic lines, often came to a violent end, and whole areas of inland territory were abandoned as entire aristocrat-dominated communities moved into the big cities.

Roman annals record, for example, the case of a Sabine named Actus Clausus. He was an ancestor of the famous Appius Claudius: 'powerful because of his wealth and celebrated for his extraordinary physical strength, but who stood out amongst his fellow men above all through his reputation for virtue and his oratorical powers'. In 504 BC, Actus Clausus moved to Rome apparently because of internal rivalries in his home town. Plutarch says that he gathered together a body of five thousand families and that he was well received in Rome by Publicola, who immediately granted the families citizens' rights, and gave to each of them two *iugera* of farmland (about 0.5 hectares or 6000 square yards) by the river Aniene. To Actus Clausus, on the other hand, he gave twenty-five *iugera*, and immediately had him admitted to membership of the Senate – the principal organ of government. In spite of the legendary overtones of the story, its significance is quite clear. The population of a city-state was being increased by the peaceful method of absorbing a whole aristocrat-dominated community. The class privileges of its 'chief' were acknowledged and he joined the council of the *patres*, while his subordinates enjoyed civil rights and were granted land to guarantee them a living.

Actus Clausus belonged to the landed aristocracy – a class which seems to have played a pre-eminent role in the Roman state, but its interests clashed with those of a new and more enterprising social group, whose economic power was based not only on land but also on money and goods acquired by means of trade. The rise of this plebeian class was effectively halted by the slump in trade which hit Rome and the coastal cities of Etruria about 470 BC, after the battle of Cumae. During the fifth century and at the beginning of the fourth, the plebeians in Rome were involved in a struggle against the patricians, and the rights which they sought to have recognized were finally granted in 367–366 BC; but the two-class society with its conflicting interests was to persist in Etruscan cities.

It is only in colonial settlements – especially those in Emilia (Marzabotto and Spina) – that the structure of the city area can provide evidence to suggest that the largest single social group consisted of an economically productive class which made its living by means of trade by land and sea.

Etruscan territorial expansion into northern Italy received its impetus from inland cities such as Perugia (according to literary sources) and Orvieto, Chiusi and Volterra (to judge from archaeological evidence). This new territory was particularly suitable for the new, rising social class to carry on certain kinds of trade, and so its members left the inland cities to the unopposed control of the landed aristocracy.

Nobles and Slaves

When the Etruscan dynasty in Rome came to an end, the state seems to have concentrated its attention on the region of Latium, where it was to make successive territorial conquests. The king's functions in public office within the state became purely religious, and political power was held first by one and then by two magistrates: the consuls of the future.

As far as the social and political structure of Etruria is concerned, and especially its state institutions, there is insufficient evidence from inscriptions and literary sources to provide a clear picture of Etruscan society from the fourth century until the time when the Etruscan states were absorbed into the Roman Republic.

The economic crisis which occurred in the fifth century was mainly concerned with trade, and probably caused the urban aristocracy to take a new look at the economic prospects of agriculture. This is suggested by the land reclamation and irrigation which the city of Veii carried out in the fifth century in its rural territory. But no plebeian class emerged alongside the landed class, as happened in Rome. On the contrary, all the written sources agree that Etruria had a 'noble' class (*principes* in Latin, *despótai* in Greek) on the one hand,

Bronze axe from Chiusi (seventh century BC; Museo Archeologico, Florence). The various kinds of axe which occur so frequently in the richly furnished tombs of this period in northern Etruria were probably symbols of political rank.

and a subservient class (*servi* in Latin, *oikétai* in Greek) on the other.

State institutions were organized more or less as follows: supreme political power within the state was held by the king (there was a king at Caere at the end of the fifth century, and although there ceased to be a king at Veii in 432 BC, the office was reinstated thirty years later), or by the *princeps civitatis*, the chief magistrate of the state. In other words, political power at city-state level was concentrated in the hands of a single magistrate. Similarly, at federal level, the assembly of the twelve Etruscan peoples appointed a single magistrate to take over as commander-in-chief of the army when necessary. In 413 BC, for example, the post was held by Velthur Spurinna, a noble from Tarquinia, who led an Etruscan contingent to Sicily to aid Athens in the siege of Syracuse.

While the class of *principes* was a small one, there was a substantial slave class which occasionally gained historical limelight in its fight for certain rights. There is evidence of a revolt at Arezzo in the mid-fourth century and another in 301 BC, and later uprisings were reported at Volsinii, Roselle and the unidentified city of Oinarea. Those involved were probably urban slaves, whose standard of living was quite different from that of country slaves. According to a Greek philosopher of the second century BC, the former were quite well educated and well dressed, whereas the latter are described by Livy as semi-barbarians. It was the urban slave class in the inland cities of Etruria who rose up in

In the first half of the sixth century BC, the terracotta frieze plaques used to decorate sacred and secular buildings show scenes from the life of the upper classes.
Above: Plaque from the temple on the Acropolis at Veii (Museo di Villa Giulia, Rome), showing a warrior in the act of mounting a chariot. His armour is of Greek type. Scenes of this kind are very common at this period, even on objects intended for quite different purposes.
Below: Plaque from the 'palace' of Murlo (Palazzo Comunale, Siena), showing two seated 'dynasts'. They hold the insignia of their rank and are served by two standing slaves.

rebellion at the end of the fourth and the beginning of the third century in order to improve their social position; but it was not until the second century, when the countryside around Chiusi and Perugia was resettled by groups of literate farming families who revitalized the agriculture of the area, that substantial results were achieved by the slave risings, which broke out again in 196 BC.

The Etruscan word used to indicate the social position of the slave in this region is *lautni*. This term is related to the word *lautn* meaning 'family', and shows that a slave was an integral part of the property of the family in its role as basic productive unit. When slaves were freed in Roman times, they were called *liberti*, and since, like everyone else of slave rank, they had no family name but were simply known at their place of work by their personal name, they took their father's personal name as a family name when they were freed.

A much larger social class was that of freemen. They had no political rights, their legal status being one which Dionysius of Halicarnassus compared to that of the underprivileged natives or *penesti* of Thessaly. More than twenty per cent of second-century funerary inscriptions refer to people of this class, who are designated by means of a name formula which does not fit into the typical Etruscan aristocratic name system, but is rather the name of an individual person, such as *Tite* (Titus) or *Cae* (Caius) and so on. These people, then, did not belong to the nobility, for they had no family name. As the Romans said of the *plebs*: *gentem non habent* – 'they do not belong to a family'. Their civil rights were probably recognized after the revolts of 196 BC when mass recognition was given to a whole social class, to whom in the past civil rights had only been granted on an individual basis. Now they were all obliged to choose a family name of a kind different from that used by the old-established aristocracy.

Right: Funerary stele of Avile Tite, from Volterra (circa 540–520 BC; Museo Guarnacci, Volterra). The inscribed dedication and the military insignia (spear and sword) identify the man as a 'chief'.

Left, above: Procession on a sarcophagus from Tuscania (second century BC; Musei Vaticani), showing a magistrate in a carriage.

Left, below: Tomba Giglioli at Tarquinia (circa 300 BC). The devices of the boar and surveyor's level which can be seen on the shields also appear on contemporary Tarquinian coins.

Preceding pages: Tomba della Caccia e Pesca at Tarquinia 530 BC). The banqueting scene is another motif whose original purpose in tomb paintings is the symbolic representation of aristocratic opulence. Differences of social rank are conveyed here by means of the different sizes of the figures.

Inland Etruria provides us with a good deal of evidence about the social status of the lower classes and their partial emancipation, which may have had quite a considerable effect on land use. The cities of southern Etruria, on the other hand, provide us with much more information about state institutions from the fourth century onwards. In this region the aristocracy seems to have been much less willing to grant rights to the slave class (who very rarely appear in funerary inscriptions); and the farm labourers must have been largely foreign slaves bought in eastern markets, of the kind mentioned by Plutarch in his life of Tiberius Graccus.

Unfortunately, the available evidence does not provide us with an overall picture of Etruscan state institutions. The Etruscan word for what Latin writers called *princeps civitatis* seems to be *zilat(h)* or *zilac(h)* – a term used to indicate a magistrate who, in mid-fourth-

Above: Relief on an urn from Volterra (late second century BC*; Museo Guarnacci, Volterra), showing armed men meeting. Preparations for the journey to the next world are represented symbolically by this meeting between a military commander and a band of armed men followed by two horn players and two more soldiers.*

Right: Relief on an urn from Volterra (first half of the first century BC*; Museo Guarnacci, Volterra). On the left is a podium with three empty chairs. Then comes the head of a procession led by two lictors. The central (headless) figure in the procession carries a scroll in his hand, and is presumably a judiciary official – that is to say an Etruscan member of the board of chief magistrates in the* municipium *of Volterra, which was now under Roman rule.*

century Tarquinia, was appointed on an annual basis. The name of the magistrate was used to indicate the year, as in the case of Roman consuls, and the post could be held when quite young, and more than once. The title *zilath*, however, had a series of attributes (*marunuch-va, cechaneri, parchis, eterau*) which suggest that, in the case of Tarquinia, there was a body of magistrates, each of whom had his own duties and responsibilities, rather like the Athenian archons. One may perhaps have had responsibility for young people (*zilath eterau* – if *eterau* means 'young'). Another, *zilc marunuch-va*, may have been in charge of other bodies of magistrates (if *marunu* is the equivalent of the Latin *quaestor*). At national level, there was the position of *zilath mechl rasnal* – a magistrate who was elected by the federal assembly at the sanctuary of Voltumna. The Latin term for this magistrate was *praetor Etruriae*, and the term *praetor* should be taken here in its basic sense of *prae-itor*: 'the one who goes in front' or 'the one who comes first'. Other titles given to magistrates were *eprthne* and *marunu*. It is quite likely that the second of these indicates financial responsibilities rather like those of a Roman *quaestor*.

To sum up, then, the Etruscan states at the end of the fifth century had one magistrate who was entrusted with political and perhaps judicial power, as well as a series of secondary magistrates with administrative responsibilities. The supreme magistrate was elected from within a small group of those of the highest rank (what Roman writers called the *ordo principum*), and there was also an assembly of elders who had a consultative role like that of a senate. (In the case of Arezzo, literary sources refer to a body of *patres* of the most important family groups.)

In other words, the institutions of the Etruscan states must have been roughly similar to those of Rome before 367 BC; that is to say, before the *plebs* finally gained substantial political influence by ensuring that one of the two highest state positions, that of consul, was reserved for a plebeian.

The Etruscan Economy

In the last chapter, particular attention was paid to the role of the family in Etruscan society, and it was shown that, in spite of subsequent transformations, it persisted as the basic productive unit, especially in agriculture. That is not to deny, of course, that the characteristics of the family as an institution changed in the course of history.

Iron Age villages, with their tribal structure, were tied to a subsistence economy in which everything was produced and consumed within the community itself. Sufficient food, tools and clothes were produced within the village to satisfy the material needs of the families which went to make it up. The next period, however, brought contact with Greek colonies and their cultures, with the result that forms of production became diversified, and the division of labour was based on different special skills in such a way that the various areas of activity were complementary. Specialization led to an increase in production, and so a use inevitably had to be found for surpluses. Now authority moved away from the father of a family to someone outside the family, who used his power to claim a share of surpluses. These went to enhance his own personal prestige, to be redistributed amongst groups who lacked this or that commodity, or else to be exchanged with other persons of equal rank. This was the period when power was in the hands of an aristocracy. There followed a period of urban civilization in which the new city-state was in effect a development from the earlier system, for it controlled the various forms of production and attributed to individual 'leaders' and landowners

Carts were among the earliest means of transport, and miniature models have been found in tombs as early as the Iron Age. This one comes from Tarquinia (Museo Archeologico, Florence).

45

certain rights denied to the lower classes, who lacked any means of production – especially land. The preservation of these rights was guaranteed to landowners by the state as emanating from the state, as can be seen from the existence of such institutions as the council of 'leaders' or the governing magistrature, both of which were a direct form of expression of the ruling class.

Within this general scheme of things, there are basically three important aspects of the economy whose development can be traced. They are: agriculture and the problems of land ownership; crafts in relation to the division of labour; and trade as a means of using up surpluses.

Agriculture and Land Ownership

The current tendency to see the Etruscans as a people dedicated to piracy – an activity which was really a form of maritime trade in the ancient world – has perhaps led to the role of their farming being underestimated. In fact farming had a basic part to play in the development of Etruscan civilization. Some indication, after all, of the origins of urbanization can be seen in the rites accompanying the foundation of an Etruscan city, as reported by the Romans. The site of the perimeter walls, we are told, was marked out with a bronze ploughshare, and an offering of first fruits and vegetables was made in the *mundus* or sacrificial trench, which thereby became an important sacred place for the citizens. This suggests a form of society which, although now sedentary, saw the tilling of the soil as what basically brought men together.

One can also see how closely urbanization was related to land ownership by looking at some late but significant literary sources, which attribute the nature and extent of private property to legendary figures.

Tarchon, the legendary founder of Tarquinia, surrounded his farmland with hedges of white vine in order to protect them from Jupiter's thunderbolts. Although his action was ostensibly aimed at warding off the wrath of the gods, it also involved marking out the boundaries of his fields, and this was felt to contribute to the organization of society itself.

There is a text in the Latin collection of the *Gromatici veteres* in which the nymph Vegoia, one of the divinities responsible for 'revealing' knowledge to the Etruscans, expresses herself quite clearly in this same connection:

Vegoia to Arruns Veltumnus.

Know that the sea was once separate from the sky. When Jupiter thereafter claimed the land of Etruria for himself, he laid down and commanded that its fields should be measured and the boundaries of cultivated areas marked out. Knowing the greed of men and their desire for land, he insisted that all should be divided up and boundaries marked out.

The time shall come, however, towards the end of the eighth century, when someone shall be overcome with greed and shall interfere with the divisions and with what has been granted, and men shall illegally interfere with, touch and move the stones which mark the boundaries. But whosoever shall touch them or move them in order to increase his own property and diminish that of others shall be punished.

If it is done by slaves, their condition shall be made worse; if they do it with the complicity of their master, his house shall soon suffer ruin and all his race shall perish.

The guilty shall be afflicted with terrible ills and diseases, which will reduce them to a state of

utter physical debility. The earth shall be rent with storms and floods which shall throw it into complete confusion. Crops shall be damaged by rain and hail, dried up by the heat of the sun and destroyed by mildew. There will be great civil strife. Know that this will happen when crimes of this kind are committed. Therefore you must not be false or speak with two tongues. Retain these teachings in your memory.

The historical situation which gave rise to this document has been identified. In 90 BC Rome wished to organize a fresh distribution of land, thereby putting at serious risk the system of colonization which had been set up in the countryside around Chiusi and Perugia during the second century. After a series of social conflicts, the cultivation of the land in these two areas was entrusted to men who were partly of the slave class. And the date specified in the text, 'the end of the eighth century', seems to correspond, in the Etruscan time scale, to what we would call the beginning of the first century BC.

The view of the world revealed in this prophecy is quite clear. The cosmic order which succeeded chaos was willed by the supreme god Tinia (the Etruscan equivalent of Jupiter), and its reflection on earth is another kind of order, in the specific form of land divisions. Anyone who upsets this order sets in motion a process which will successively undermine the equilibrium of society not only at a personal and family level, but also at an economic and political level. The right to property is established by laws which are immutable because divinely willed; and the physical symbols of this right are boundary stones. Therefore they must not be moved. In fact there are plenty of second-century boundary stones in inland Etruria with inscriptions indicating territory subject to the

Right: Stone cippus, *used to indicate the boundary of a country estate near Perugia. The long text engraved on it provides evidence of an agreement as to possession of the land after a quarrel between the* Afuna *and* Velthina *families of Perugia (second century* BC*; Museo Archeologico, Perugia).*

Left: Bronze plough from Talamone (Museo Archeologico, Florence). This votive model is complete in all its parts, including the yoke. It was part of a hoard of bronze objects found near the site of the famous battle between Gauls and Romans in 225 BC.

jurisdiction of the nation (*tular raśnal* 'boundaries of Etruria'), the city-state (*tular spural* 'city boundaries') or individuals (*tular alfil* 'boundaries of the property of the Alfii').

The situation described above occurred, of course, at a particular moment in history, but it must have been preceded by a long period of evolution both in land ownership rights and in the relationship between landowners and workers, whose existence as distinct social classes is confirmed by the text of Vegoia's prophecy.

This process began when towns came into being, and probably goes back to the time when the Etruscans first came into contact with Greek settlers. Before the existence of towns, farming may well have been an uncertain occupation, dependent upon the natural produce of the land. The land, in other words, may have been used only for what it produced of its own accord. It was probably contact with Greek settlers which brought in a system of farming based on ploughing and allowing fields to lie fallow for a year or more, during which time they might have a secondary role for growing vegetables or as pasture. At this stage of development, it was clearly not enough to own a single piece of land and, in addition, it became necessary to mark the boundary between cultivated and fallow fields. This was probably the time when families and communities began to quarrel over the appropriation of land, the use of slave labour and outlets for surpluses.

The technique adopted for measuring and dividing up land must have come direct from Greek settlers. This can be deduced from the fact that the name of the instrument used by Roman land surveyors was *groma*. If the word had passed directly into Latin from Greek, it would have become *gnoma*; and the change from *gn* to *gr* can be related to the etruscanization of Greek nouns adopted in Etruria. Therefore the instrument

Above: 'Ponte Sodo' at Veii. Water from one branch of the river Cremera was channelled through this tunnel, and holes were made in the roof so that water could be drawn off from above. The construction of the tunnel was one of a number of irrigation and land reclamation projects carried out in the countryside around Veii in the fifth century BC.

Right: The famous votive bronze ploughman from Arezzo (late fifth century BC; *Museo di Villa Giulia, Rome).*

Small ivory plaque made to decorate one side of a small casket found in a tomb at Orvieto. The scene shows stag-hunting – presumably as an 'aristocratic' sport (520–500 BC; Museo Archeologico, Florence).

must have been used by the Etruscans. Even more significant, however, is the fact that when Latin literature acquired the important new genre of works on agriculture, two writers of Etruscan origin – the Sasernas, father and son – appeared on the scene at the end of the second century BC, between the two major exponents of the genre in Republican times, Cato and Varro. And they brought their own personal experience to the subject. Their ideal farm was small and self-sufficient, even to its equipment. Even the containers for foodstuffs, whether for sale or for consumption on the farm, were to be made on the spot. It is thus more than a coincidence, perhaps, that a farm of this kind, dating to the second century BC, has been found near Blera in the region of Viterbo. It even has its own kiln for making architectural terracottas. Furthermore, the farms which were scattered across the countryside in the territory of Chiusi must have been similar. With-

in these farming units everything was highly organized. A worker's productive capacity was calculated at so many days, and he and his family were subject to a very strict discipline. Thus the Sasernas were basing their theory of farming on the value, in terms of production, of the medium-sized farm at a time when the greatest threat to the farming system was the large estate.

According to classical authors, the Etruscan countryside was very rich, and in using this term they were referring to the works of man as well as to the natural fertility of the land. These 'rich fields of Etruria' (*opulenta Etruriae arva*) were remarked on by a Roman at the end of the fourth century, when he surveyed them from the summit of Monte Cimino, and they must have provided supplies for Rome in time of famine, and for the troops involved in the wars against Hannibal both in Italy and Africa. When Diodorus Siculus borrowed a description written by a late second-century Greek

Scene from the Tomba della Caccia e Pesca at Tarquinia (540–530 BC). It forms part of a larger narrative fresco in a style which derives from East Greek painting. Particular attention is paid to the representation of fishing methods.

writer who had been in Italy, he was in a sense epitomizing all that has come down to us from antiquity concerning the fertility of Etruscan soil:

> The earth bears much fruit and, by the effort they put into cultivating it, the inhabitants can make it yield an abundance of produce, beyond what they require for their own sustenance. . . . The fields consist of vast plains, interspersed with many hills, and they are well cultivated. The land is fertile because it is very humid, in summer as well as in winter (*Diodorus Siculus*, V, 40).

This description seems particularly applicable to those areas crossed by streams flowing into the Tiber, whose waters were used for transporting a variety of farm produce to Rome. It applies less well to the coastal areas of Etruria, except perhaps for the Maremma plains. There is also a famous letter written by Pliny the Younger at the end of the first century AD to a friend, in which he describes the view from a villa of his in Etruria, with ploughed fields, vine-covered hills and the Tiber in the background. 'The river is navigable', he adds, 'and in winter and spring takes all kinds of crops to Rome' (*Letters*, V, 6).

Literary sources also tend to confirm archaeological evidence about the countryside around Veii. When the Gauls destroyed the city of Rome by fire at the beginning of the fourth century BC, its inhabitants actually thought of occupying the Etruscan city of Veii, which they had recently conquered, because the countryside around it was much more fertile and extensive than their own. Whether in the plain or on hillsides, the fields enjoyed a healthy climate, and there were no nearby marshes or rivers to chill the air in the morning. Instead, there were springs of pure water. This description from Livy can be related to archaeological evidence suggesting a countryside with scattered farmhouses, where man had made great efforts to construct a drainage system by drawing off water into underground channels. All this suggests a system of intensive agriculture involving such a massive transformation of the land that the state authority must surely have been directly involved.

What botanical evidence we have for the development of agriculture in Etruria from the Bronze Age onwards comes from Monte Cetona – an area which certainly lent itself to the development of various types of farming. Cereals were grown at the foot of the mountain, in what was later to be the rich territory of Chiusi, while sheep and cattle were reared on the mountain slopes. Given the region and the period, this kind of farming is somewhat unusual, since quality cereals such as naked wheat are the exception in the history of the subsequent period (that is, the first millennium BC), when the less valued hulled wheats predominate, especially emmer (*triticum dicoccum*). These types of corn must have been grown alongside barley and millet as well as a fairly substantial group of pulses, which evidently offered an important nutritional alternative to cereals because of their protein content. In the eighth century, it was the various kinds of hulled wheats which predominated, as, for example, at Luni sul Mignone. These were less valued and easier to grow, but at the same time a greater variety of pulses was used, including kinds which provided good forage for cattle. The fact that wheat, other cereals and pulses have been found together in food stores, provides us with direct evidence of two things. Firstly, it shows that there were sufficient calories for survival in a diet based perhaps, as in Rome, on *puls*, which was a kind of rough bread made from emmer flour boiled in water and made into a dough. And secondly, the presence of pulses shows that the fallow system was widely practised in land cultivation, with pulses and corn being

grown in rotation. Growing pulses allowed the soil to be regularly turned over, which was necessary for the sowing of corn later on.

Although emmer was not a high quality crop, it was resistant to cold, and grew even in damp or lightly prepared ground. It was resistant, so Roman agriculturalists tell us, because of the presence of the husk. Each *iugerum* of land (about 0.25 hectares or 3000 square yards) could be sown with 10 *modii* (about 87 litres or 2.5 bushels) of emmer seed. Once the crop was gathered it was parched – parching being a very ancient method of getting rid of the husk. The wheat could now be pounded, and Pliny the Elder tells us that the Etruscans had special kinds of pestle for this particular purpose. Emmer was grown principally in the countryside around Chiusi, but we have evidence that the more highly valued wheats such as *siligo* were grown at Arezzo and Pisa as well as at Chiusi for making sweeter and better-quality breads.

The grapevine was introduced into Italy by Greek settlers. Indeed the very word *vinum* (wine), used in both Etruscan and Latin, may come from the Greek *(w)oinos*. The Latin poets of the early Imperial age, however, seem to have been too intent on praising the quality of the grapes of Campania or the wine of the Po valley to bother with Etruscan wine, though Martial mentioned that it was too light. They are in any case concerned with too late a stage in vine growing for our purposes. In the fourth century BC, however, the Greeks referred to the Etruscans, men and women alike, as heavy drinkers. At the beginning of that century, so we are told, a man from Chiusi, called Arruns, persuaded the Gauls to invade Italy by enticing them with his local wine. At any rate, the system of vine growing which one finds in sixth- and fifth-century BC wall and vase paintings, with vines trained up high, using trees, posts or trellises as supports, may have come from the Etruscans. Certainly the use of trees and posts as supports for tall vines was to remain customary in northern Italy.

From early historical times wine seems to have been a luxury, and its use must have been somewhat restricted. In Rome, for example, its use was subject to strict laws which were supposed to go back to the time of Numa Pompilius. At the end of the eighth century and throughout the seventh, it was imported from Phoenicia and Chios, but by the end of that period there was such a surplus in home production that the wine of Vulci was exported as far as Sicily and the south coast of France.

The olive, too, was brought to Etruria by Greek settlers. In fact the Etruscan word for oil, *eleiva*, comes from Doric Greek *elaiva* (oil), and the derivation of the Latin word *amurca* (meaning marc, or the dregs of pressed olives) from the Greek *amorga* can only be accounted for by its having passed through an Etruscan

Top: Cinerary urn from Volterra (late second century BC; Museo Guarnacci, Volterra). A pastoral scene, such as the one in this relief, is unusual. In this case a shepherd is holding two horses by the bridle, and is leading a flock of sheep, pigs and cattle. These are the animals used for sacrifices at official ceremonies.

Above: Terracotta casket from Chiusi (second century BC; Museo Archeologico, Florence). In the bloodthirsty fighting scenes on the 'middle class' funerary monuments from the territory of Chiusi, the most frequently represented protagonist is a man armed with a plough. The episode probably reflects class warfare revolving around the possession of land. There are hints of this in the Roman historians, who refer to the social rebellions which took place in Etruria during 196 BC.

stage where the sound *o* became *u* and the sound *g* became *c*. Like wine, olive oil was a luxury and may have been imported from Phoenicia. Certainly it was imported into Italy and Etruria at the end of the eighth and the beginning of the seventh century. It travelled in jars made in Attica, where olives had been grown and used for making oil since very ancient times, going back to the legendary story of the founding of Athens. It was probably later that olives came to be grown in Etruria, but olive stones were preserved in a vessel in a tomb at Cerveteri dating to as early as 580–560 BC.

Olive and vine growing, then, became fundamentally important in Etruria, and there is no doubt that all the advice on the subject provided by Roman writers on agriculture of the second and first century BC was based partly on lengthy experience, leading to the recognition that these particular products were luxury foods. It is also probable that the element of commercial speculation involved in vine growing and the export of surpluses played a part in attracting certain specific interests to land and land ownership.

Farming also involved keeping animals. Oxen were used to till the land and so cannot have been a major source of food. The Roman agriculturalist Columella says that, in Etruria and Latium, oxen were lean, but hard workers, and there is no doubt that their reputation for stamina derived from the nine ploughings which were the rule in Etruscan fields. Pigs, on the other hand, did provide a basic food, and pork was also eaten dried. The slaughter of pigs was sometimes connected with specific ancient ceremonies, such as the marriages of kings and dignitaries. Little is known about sheep, though they too must have been very important. There must also have been selective breeding of horses, even in Archaic times. Work horses or those kept for their meat were considered of inferior breed, whereas horses intended for use in war or for riding (an art which developed in the seventh century) seem to have had different physical characteristics in that they were thinner.

We can see that agriculture played a vital part in the Etruscan economy. Methods of land cultivation seem to have developed hand in hand with changes in social relationships. What completely upset the self-sufficient economy of Iron Age villages was the division of land, the first symptom of which was the introduction of the fallow system; and the subsequent advent of the vine and the olive caused agriculture not only to become even more specialized but also to acquire commercial possibilities. The concept of private property with fixed boundaries, as propounded by Vegoia, and the system of medium-sized farm units worked by slave labour, as set out in the treatises of the Sasernas, are evidence that the division and cultivation of the land reflect divisions within the society.

Arts and Crafts

It is commonly supposed that one of the principal purposes of the Greek colonization of Campania was, at least in the initial stages, to safeguard regular supplies of minerals from Etruria. The truth of this supposition seems to be confirmed by two facts which have only recently been discovered. Firstly, when the Euboeans established their first trading post in Ischia, and later (about the middle of the eighth century) founded a colony at Cumae, they already had their own metal industry, which made use of iron ore deposits in their home country. Secondly, analysis of a mineral found in the form of ore in Ischia has shown it to be hematite from the island of Elba.

Our knowledge of the island of Elba and its minerals in ancient times comes partly from remarks made by

View of the island of Elba – rich in iron mines and furnaces used in the first stages of smelting. The area comprising Elba and the Piombino promontory (where the city of Populonia stood) was for a long time the ultimate goal of Greek colonists in search of raw materials. Hence the creation of blacksmiths' quarters for smelting iron ore from the sixth century BC onwards.

The map overleaf shows the distribution of mineral deposits in Etruria.

53

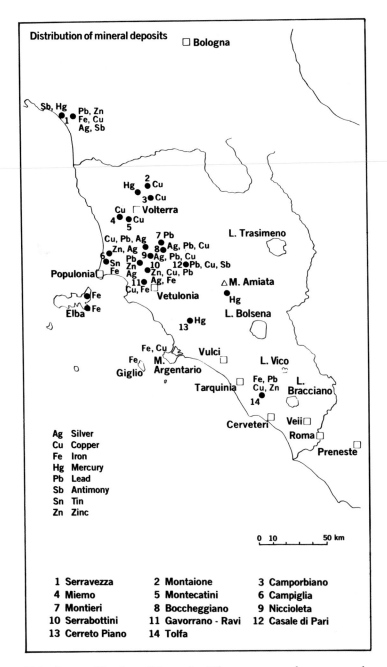

Distribution of mineral deposits

☐ Bologna

Sb, Hg ● 1 ● Pb, Zn
         Fe, Cu
         Ag, Sb

Hg ● 2 ● Cu
       3 ● Cu
Cu ☐ Volterra
4 ● ● Cu
   5
Cu, Pb, Ag   7 Pb
● Zn, Ag   8 ● Ag, Pb, Cu
6 ●   Pb 9 ● Ag, Pb, Cu
  ● Sn Zn ● 10   12 ● Pb, Cu, Sb
Populonia ☐ Fe Ag ● Zn, Cu, Pb
         11 ● Ag, Fe
         Cu, Fe
         ● Fe   Vetulonia
Elba ● Fe   13 ● Hg

L. Trasimeno

△ M. Amiata
● Hg

L. Bolsena

Fe, Cu
Fe ● M.   Vulci ☐
Giglio ● Argentario   L. Vico
                 Fe, Pb
Tarquinia ☐   Cu, Zn   L. Bracciano
           14 ●
Cerveteri ☐   Veii ☐
         Roma ☐
              Preneste ☐

Ag Silver
Cu Copper
Fe Iron
Hg Mercury
Pb Lead
Sb Antimony
Sn Tin
Zn Zinc

0 10   50 km

1 Serravezza   2 Montaione   3 Camporbiano
4 Miemo   5 Montecatini   6 Campiglia
7 Montieri   8 Boccheggiano   9 Niccioleta
10 Serrabottini   11 Gavorrano - Ravi 12 Casale di Pari
13 Cerreto Piano 14 Tolfa

Diodorus Siculus (V, 13). They are perhaps worth setting out in full:

> Near the city of Populonia there is an island called *Aithaleia*. It is about 100 stades from the coast, and was given its name because of the smoke (*aithalos* in Greek) which completely envelops it. For the island is rich in siderite, which is broken up for smelting, to secure the iron contained in it in large quantities. Those who carry out this work crush the stone and bake it in specially constructed furnaces. The heat causes the metal to liquefy in the furnaces and it is then shaped into ingots of medium size which look like large sponges in form. Large quantities of these ingots can be bought from those who deal in them, and they transport them as far as Dicaearcheia [Roman Puteoli; modern Pozzuoli] or other trading stations.

So we see that the iron refining industry was already important in Elba in the first century BC, and involved both smelters and merchants. But there had also been similar furnaces at Populonia. Permanent workshops had been set up in the fourth century in the area outside the town previously occupied by large tombs. Thus when, at the end of the first century BC, the Greek geographer Strabo looked down from the citadel on the promontory, he could see amongst other things the furnaces in which iron from Elba was smelted.

The distribution of metal ores in Tuscany, as well as traces of ancient mines and furnaces, make it clear that iron was not the only metal to be mined. Copper was also mined to a considerable extent, and perhaps tin as well – these two metals being the ingredients of bronze (an alloy consisting almost invariably of 86 per cent copper and 14 per cent tin). Indeed, the Greek settlers found that the Etruscans were by no means entirely inexperienced in working metals. The manufacture of bronze tools and personal ornaments was part of a tradition which was already well established by the Late Bronze Age. At that time only groups of crafts-men-merchants were involved, and they probably operated outside the community by travelling around a certain limited area. Since iron was basic to the manu-facture of tools for digging and cutting, its use became of vital importance when farming was rationalized and intensified, but we do not know whether tools were manufactured in the vicinity of the mines them-selves. There are no farm implements in tombs, but what has been found there shows that iron was used for cartwheels, spits, fire-irons, axes, knives and sometimes objects for personal use as well. In the seventh and early sixth century, for example, there is specific evidence from the inland part of northern Etruria for the use of iron for *niello* decoration on buckles and parts of bronze war chariots.

The setting up of permanent sites for the metal industry was almost certainly a result of the concentra-tion of the population in the major towns, when the manufacturing industry became an essential factor in the division of labour; and there is no doubt that, at an early stage, artisan activities were to be found prin-cipally in those towns which were nearest to the ores. An example is Vetulonia, situated close to the Colline Metallifere. One of the most widely used methods of working metal, from the Iron Age onwards, was cold hammering, using cast bronze in bars or leaf. This technique persisted amongst the metalworkers, especi-ally in the manufacture of domestic containers, the various parts of the outside being joined together with small bronze rivets rather than by welding, which came later.

For obvious reasons, there is a whole area of craft activity using organic materials such as textiles and wood for which archaeological evidence is lacking. Hence

Right: The working of metals became widespread among the Etruscans from the early Iron Age. This razor from Vetulonia (eighth century BC) is unusal in that it bears an incised hunting scene (Museo Archeologico, Grosseto).

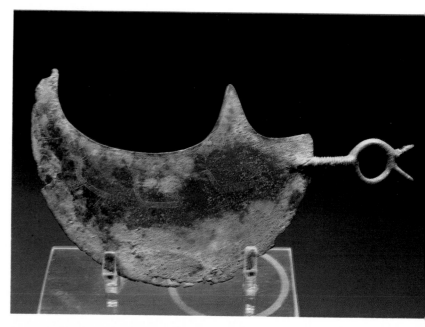

Below: Bronze jug with a pointed spout (Museo Archeologico, Florence). In the sixth and fifth centuries BC Etruscan bronzes were sufficiently famous to be praised by Attic poets. This example is typical of a category of bronze vessel which was widely exported north of the Apennines and even beyond the Alps. In the latter area such prestige goods were much sought after by Celtic 'chiefs'.

it is pottery above all else on which archaeology is obliged to concentrate its attention. Since pottery is capable of long survival in the earth, it acts as a kind of 'type fossil' in archaeological studies. The nature of vases as consumer goods, however, provides us with important information about both pottery techniques and the relationships, within the pottery industry, between various kinds of product made for different purposes and for customers of different social standing.

Here again, contact with the most up-to-date Greek potters was of vital importance. In the Iron Age, pottery for ordinary use was normally made with fairly impure impasto clay. Pottery was produced within the village and formed part of the self-sufficient economy which was characteristic of the period. Then, in the second half of the eighth century, Greek settlers introduced containers of more functional shape, made from purified and waterproofed clay. They were shaped on a wheel and decorated with mineral paints. These foreign craftsmen provided the impetus for the setting up of workshops devoted entirely to this kind of finer pottery, in direct imitation of Greek imports. Thus the Etruscan names for containers remain close to the equivalent Greek term: *qutum* (jug) comes from the Greek *kothon, thina* (type of pot) from *dinos, aska* (small flask) from *askos*, and so on.

Until the end of the fifth century, the demand for pottery was partly satisfied by imports from Greece for wealthy customers, and partly by local products, which copied Greek shapes and decoration in a pedestrian fashion.

In the seventh and the first half of the sixth century, Corinthian pottery held sway, whereas Attic pottery predominated between 550 and 450 BC. By now, however, local potteries were organized on Greek lines and established themselves in Etruscan cities – notably

while decoration was occasionally painted on, it often took the form of relief. About half way through the seventh century, shiny black vases began to be produced in direct imitation of metalware. This was *bucchero* which, for 150 years or more, constituted a typically Etruscan product.

It is pottery in particular, then, and the way it developed in the seventh century, which allows us to draw a vitally important conclusion about the organization of craft activities. We find, that is to say, that specialized products were created which were only partly influenced by Iron Age traditions, because the taste of the more influential classes was better satisfied with what could be achieved by taking advantage of the latest technical advances made by Greek craftsmen.

It can be said of metallurgy and even more so of the art of decorating metalwork and engraving precious substances (ivory and amber) that the seventh century saw the birth of what one might call artistic crafts, with the production of luxury goods for an élite. There were no changes in the techniques used for working metal, although the influence of the orientalizing style did have some effect on decoration, but fairly limited local centres for metalworking and engraving came into being as a result of the import of bronzes from Asia, ivories from northern Syria and Phoenician objects made of precious metals with repoussé decoration. Even though the goods these centres produced were destined for the wealthy classes and therefore limited in scope, it is possible to trace their chronological development.

At a time when society was in a state of flux, but where groups of nobles held a dominant position, the social status of the craftsman was certainly not a minor one. Thus when Greek settlers join Etruscan communities, artisans as well as merchants are noticeable amongst them, and this seems to have been a period when crafts-

Vulci – thereby effectively constituting a pottery industry, which produced imitation Corinthian from 630 to 550 BC and imitation East Greek in the second half of the sixth century. In the fifth century, there was sporadic imitation of Attic red-figure pottery, and in the fourth century (by which time Attic pottery was no longer imported) local workshops producing figured pottery took on a new lease of life and established themselves in the major cities (Cerveteri, Tarquinia, Vulci, Orvieto, Chiusi and Volterra).

Figured pottery was something of a luxury and was obviously kept for important occasions, but from the seventh century onwards there were various kinds of more ordinary pottery which had developed out of Iron Age products. Techniques were refined; the potter's wheel came into general use, clays of different colours were used, surfaces were stick burnished, and

Left: Small bronze flask from Vulci (Museo di Villa Giulia, Rome). Repoussé decoration on metal occurs very early, both on weapons and utensils found in warriors' tombs. This drinking flask, intended for a man, dates to the end of the eighth century BC.

Right: Ostrich egg (first half of the seventh century BC; Museo Nazionale, Tarquinia). The egg came from Egypt and was painted in Etruria; the decoration imitates the Greek Geometric style. With the addition of attachments (mouth, base, handle) in other materials, such eggs were turned into vessels for holding liquids.

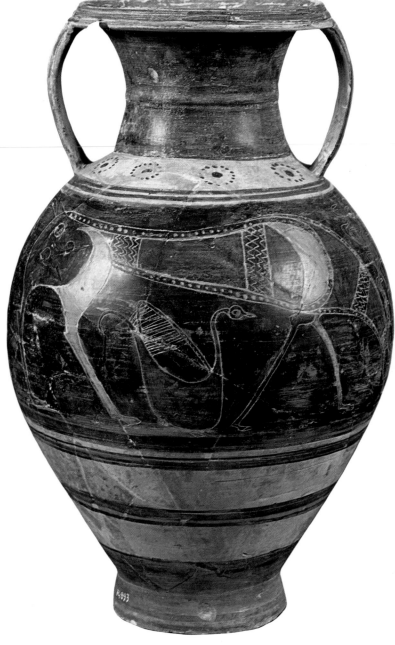

Above, left: Euboean krater from Pescia Romana (circa 720 BC; Museo Archeologico, Grosseto). One of the most splendid examples of Greek Late Geometric pottery imported into Etruria. A luxury item probably brought to the west by the Euboeans who founded colonies around the Bay of Naples, it was used for serving wine.

Above right: 'Polychrome' amphora (Museo di Villa Giulia, Rome). Between 630 and 550 BC there grew up in Etruria a great many pottery workshops which used Greek styles of decoration in order to satisfy a widespread demand. The Geometric style now gives way to a new animal style of decoration, deriving from East Greek and Corinthian models. The group of 'Polychrome Vases', produced between 630 and 600 BC, is unusual, however; it shows that some potters and painters went beyond the purely imitative routine activities of their contemporaries.

men had an above average education; for example, they often signed the objects they made. Inscriptions on vases are usually expressed in the first person, and frequently take the form of a brief statement such as: 'I am Lemausna's jug. Ranazu shaped me', 'I was designed by Aranth', 'I was made by Larthuza Kulenie' and so on. It is likely that the social role of the craftsman changed as his function within the urban community changed. At first craftsmen were part of the entourage of the 'chiefs', and they occupied a very special position because they made things specifically for richer customers.

Specialization, however, and the fact that there was an increase in finished products for a more general urban public, brought about divisions among craftsmen, which ancient writers present as actually taking the form of guilds. The existence of craft guilds in Rome, for example, was supposed to go back to the time of Numa Pompilius, though nowadays it tends to be associated with the time of the growth of Rome under Servius Tullius (second quarter of the sixth century), and there is no doubt that in the culturally more advanced Etruscan cities the same sort of thing may have been going on at the same time. The list of Roman guilds, as provided by Plutarch (*Life of Numa Pompilius*, 17), contains nine categories of craftsmen: flute-players, goldsmiths, masons, dyers, shoemakers, tanners, leather-workers, bronze-workers and potters. It includes certain Etruscan crafts which have already been mentioned (goldsmiths, bronze-workers and potters) and one must add blacksmiths, who certainly existed in some towns. As for the other crafts mentioned, the fact that Etruscan shoes, known as *calcei*, were highly regarded in Rome leads to the supposition that there were also Etruscan leather-workers, and it seems likely that there were also dyers, because Etruscan nobles used purple a great deal and molluscs were cultivated along the Tyrrhenian coast from Porto Ercole in late Republican times. The guild of flute-players is certainly an ancient one, for there are no figured monuments from the mid-seventh century onwards which do not depict the straight flute being played in sacred or private ceremonies.

There is archaeological evidence that further specialization took place within the guilds. About 580 BC, for example, a group of craftsmen came into existence who were concerned almost exclusively with making ornamental terracottas for private houses and sanctuaries. Tarquinius Priscus, the first Etruscan king of Rome, apparently sent for a famous sculptor named Vulca from Veii, in order to get him to make the sacred terracotta statue which was to be placed in the temple of Jupiter on the Capitol. This temple was in fact inaugurated in 507 BC – in the early years of the Republic – and the two Tarquins had taken steps to ensure that it should have typically Etruscan characteristics both in plan and elevation, and they were particularly careful to see that the statues for its upper decoration were sculpted personally by artists from Veii.

The high quality of Etruscan craftsmanship at the time when urban culture was at its most advanced became almost a commonplace among classical writers. Frequent references are made to luxury vases in repoussé gold and silver, special ornaments such as crowns of gold leaves and various bronze articles. These include lamps and, more importantly, bronze statues, some of which were placed in Roman sanctuaries. A few of these have survived, such as the Chimera from Arezzo and the Mars from Todi, which was probably made at Orvieto. When the Romans sacked Volsinii in 264 BC, their booty included two thousand bronze statues, and Marcus Fulvius Flaccus, the man responsible for the enterprise, was able to dedicate an offering including

These two vases were decorated by East Greek artists who emigrated from their homeland after the Persian invasions and settled in Etruria between 540 and 520 BC. Such craftsmen must in fact have constituted a very important means of cultural transmission during the fresh wave of Hellenization which reached Etruria around the second half of the sixth century BC.

Top: Detail of a black-figure hydria *depicting the apotheosis of Hercules (from Cerveteri circa 530 BC; Museo di Villa Giulia, Rome).*

Above: Black-figure dinos *showing a youth between sirens (from Cerveteri circa 530 BC; Museo di Villa Giulia, Rome).*

a number of bronze votive images, in the Forum Boarium in Rome.

There is plenty of evidence for trading in finished objects, especially bronzes, at the end of the sixth and the beginning of the fifth century. Jugs with pointed spouts, probably made at Vulci, were sold beyond the Alps, perhaps by way of the emporium at Spina. Fairly simple small jugs with handles reached Sicily and Corsica. And one of the famous bronze tripods, works of art perhaps made at Vulci, was discovered as far away as the acropolis of Athens.

Works of art are, of course, craft products. To what extent they were produced in towns it is impossible to say, because so little research into towns has been carried out. Certainly great care was taken over the decoration of sacred buildings, the principal decorative materials were light, such as terracotta, with bronze and terracotta votive offerings; but the most striking objects were those made for tomb furnishings and decoration. Here again, contact with Greek culture was fundamentally important, for the various styles current in different periods in the history of Hellenic art had a profound influence on Etruscan figurative art. It is true to say that from the earliest period of urban culture, the groups of craftsmen working in the various towns enjoyed periods of fruitful contact with their Greek counterparts, followed by periods of complete stagnation when the contacts were reduced or cut off. It is almost as though Greek art were something very distant, which only reached and influenced the various regions of Etruria at certain moments in history. At such moments it set in motion a process which came to a halt as soon as factors quite unrelated to artistic matters caused these contacts to decrease. And the purpose of art objects, intended as they were for an aristocratic élite, reflects changes in taste and the varying wealth of buyers.

There is no doubt, for example, that it was contact with East Greek artists in the second half of the sixth century which instilled a new vitality into Etruscan figurative art. The taste for large pictures, both in public buildings at Cerveteri and the painted tombs of Tarquinia, arose from direct contact with artists from Clazomenae, Phocaea and Samos (Greek cities on the coast of present day Turkey), who emigrated across the Mediterranean after the Persian invasions and settled at the emporium of Gravisca, near Tarquinia. The battle of Cumae (*circa* 470 BC) severed these contacts and it is difficult to find anything at a later date in the towns along the coast which directly reflects the great classical art of Greece. Only well into the fourth century came another improvement in quality, stimulated by important work in the figurative arts in Taranto; but another period of stagnation followed in the third century. Then again, the thriving 'mass production' of funerary urns in northern Etruria in the second

The makers of terracottas were among the most famous Etruscan craftsmen. This antefix with the head of a Silenus was used in the decoration of Temple A at Pyrgi (circa 460 BC; Museo di Villa Giulia, Rome).

century coincided with a period when the population and economy of the towns were expanding, thereby providing a basis for increased craft activity, including the production of art objects for a special class of customer.

It is nowadays pointless to attempt to assess Etruscan artistic culture by appending comprehensive labels. Behind all artistic phenomena, especially in peripheral areas, lie the complex workings of history, which have to be assessed in all their chronological and geographical aspects. Any judgment made on this basis must take into account a whole variety of factors, amongst which are the way the production of works of art was organized and the public for whom they were intended, for they form part of a framework which in many ways exerted a determining influence.

Trade and Piracy

It is only recently that Etruscologists have become interested in problems of 'commerce', and indeed the term itself might seem ambiguous in its modernity, if it were not taken to include all forms of trading in merchandise. And the term 'merchandise' must also be taken in the broadest sense, to include goods of any kind produced by human labour which become involved in a trading process and acquire a different value according to the different time and place of their existence.

In studying ancient 'commerce', there are three salient factors to be taken into account: the way goods circulate, and hence the area within which they circulate; the way their value is determined; and the actual form that trading takes.

How goods circulated depended very much on geographical factors, and there is no doubt that the position of Villanovan settlements, later to become city-states, was governed by such considerations. The sea and rivers offered natural means of communication, in the same way as on land, the ancient tracks made in moving flocks of sheep. All means of transport, from wooden boats (one of which was used as a funeral couch in an Iron Age tomb near Cerveteri) to ships (for which there is evidence in the figurative arts from the mid-seventh century), and from beasts of burden to carts, together constitute the ordinary means by which a trading economy could be carried on.

The first signs of contact with maritime traders belong to the late Iron Age (the time of the arrival of the earliest Greek settlers) when exotic objects appear in certain localities: Greek Geometric pottery at Veii, a repoussé bronze bowl of Phoenician origin at Vetulonia, and a small nuraghic (Sardinian) bronze in a tomb at Vulci. The chief attraction for foreign ships was the region rich in minerals, but if we are to assume that there was direct trading between foreign sea merchants and the local people who 'ran' the mineral deposits, we would expect to find imported goods only in the towns or ports which dealt in minerals, and therefore only at Populonia and Vetulonia. But exotic objects are also found at Veii, Tarquinia, Vulci and even in the cemeteries of Latium – all places a long way from the areas of mineral deposits. Later, in the first half of the seventh century, large quantities of luxury objects in 'princely' tombs appear not only at Vetulonia but also at Cerveteri, Tarquinia and Vulci, as well as towns in Latium, such as Castel di Decima and Palestrina (Praeneste). These luxury goods take the form of repoussé bronze weapons in the local metalworking tradition, rich personal ornaments, gold objects, and eastern ivories or local imitations made by the craftsmen already mentioned. But why should such goods be found at some distance from the rich mineral areas where the trading actually

took place? The answer is probably that goods were being appropriated in a 'predatory' manner, or else were sample deliveries, so to speak, used by the sea merchants to guarantee themselves access to the rich mineral areas. In other words, if the sea merchants wanted to reach Vetulonia or Populonia, they had to call in at other places on the way, since they could only sail small distances at a time. This is the only way one can explain the fact that in Archaic times there are numerous towns of primary or secondary importance along the Tyrrhenian coast from the mouth of the Tiber to Populonia, but none further north along the coast from Livorno to Pisa, which was founded later – perhaps at the end of the sixth century.

In the pre-urban period, when there was no established trading system recognized by a public authority, any form of trading must obviously have been intended to be to the advantage of a community or its recognized 'chief'. It is also clear, however, that the new system introduced by the Greek merchants, including trade in luxury goods, must be one of the factors, along with others already mentioned, responsible for bringing about an uneven distribution of wealth. Luxury objects became 'prestige' goods, indicative of the social standing of their owner, and they were then involved in a series of exchanges between 'chiefs' which, in their ceremonial aspect, may have constituted an effective contract designed to confirm agreements or friendships or even exchanges of a commercial kind. Indeed, the inscriptions on luxury objects themselves bear witness to the confirmation of existing relationships by means of valuable gifts. 'I am the fibula of Aranth Velavesna. Mamurke Tursikina gave (it)'; 'I am (the fibula) of Mamarce presented to Arte'. These are some of the inscriptions found on gold objects in tombs, but the practice was probably widespread throughout the seventh century, and involved luxuries of many dif–

Right: Repoussé silver mirror (second half of the fourth century BC, *from Bomarzo; Museo Archeologico, Florence). It is very unusual to find a mirror on which relief and engraved decoration appear together. Three gods are depicted here:* Aplu *(Apollo) is on the left,* Tinia *(Jupiter) with his sceptre and thunderbolt is in the centre, and* Turms *(Mercury) is on the right.*

Left: Detail of a gold ring setting (from Populonia circa 550 BC*; Museo Archeologico, Florence). Among the craftsmen who emigrated to Etruria from East Greece and Cyprus were goldsmiths and gemstone engravers, who set up their workshops in the coastal cities, especially Cerveteri, Tarquinia and Vulci.*

ferent kinds, including such goods as wine. Precious metal objects and ivories – mostly made by craftsmen at Cerveteri – become objects to be exchanged amongst the representatives of powerful groups. It is no coincidence, for instance, that many such objects have been found in the 'princely' tombs at Vetulonia – a city directly involved in the extraction of minerals. Such exchanges can only partly be described as 'commercial', because they also have a significance related to the prestige of the donor and the history of the object itself (which is why the object bears an inscription recording the name of the donor). This exchange of gifts was carried out in accordance with the classical system of reciprocity, as practised in Homeric society, but behind its ceremonial appearance there must also have been a kind of commerce in the form of straightforward bartering, primarily in relation to the raw materials which Etruria lacked. Since there were no local sources of gold, silver, ivory and amber, they were imported by land or sea to be worked locally. Dionysius of Halicarnassus (III, 46) tells of the noble Corinthian Demaratus, father of Tarquinius Priscus, who was already trading with the Etruscans in the mid seventh century 'taking Greek goods to the Etruscans and Etruscan goods to Greece', and who finally set himself up in Tarquinia, bringing artists and craftsmen with him from Greece. This story shows how easily foreigners were accepted in Etruscan society, and how easily they could be absorbed into local communities, where social organization was still very fluid. And, judging by the personal history of Tarquinius Priscus after his move to Rome, it was a society in which rapid advancement was possible.

The predominant form of trade, however, must have been piracy, and the ancient sources which refer to Etruscan 'pirates' are confirmed by archaeological evidence. The seventh Homeric hymn, for example, relates how the god Dionysus was kidnapped as a child by Tyrrhenian pirates who thought he was a king's son and therefore expected to ransom him at a handsome profit. Legend and history are blended in what we are told of the Etruscans patrolling the Tyrrhenian Sea as far as Sicily and the Balearic Islands, Sardinia and Corsica. (An Etruscan settlement dating to the fifth century has been discovered in Corsica.) The same is true of Etruscan activity in the Adriatic where, from the end of the sixth to the third century, sea traffic was under the control of enterprising Etruscan groups stationed at Adria and Spina. It is no coincidence that the Tyrrhenian Sea took its name from the Greek word for the Etruscans and that the Adriatic Sea should be named after the port of Adria.

Archaeological evidence for this kind of activity is usually sought in the distribution around the Mediterranean of specific kinds of merchandise which can be confidently identified as Etruscan, not forgetting that Etruscan trade included the export of wine and oil as well as of metals (especially iron). The cargo of an Etruscan ship which was wrecked about 580–570 BC has been found near Cap d'Antibes on the French coast between Nice and Cannes. The ship was carrying not only wine jars but also bucchero jugs and cups, as well as imitation Corinthian cups from Vulci. Thus we can deduce that there was a surplus available for export in the production of such luxuries as wine and oil (the latter contained in small jars which imitate Corinthian pottery both in shape and decoration). The Cap d'Antibes ship illustrates the wide distribution of bucchero across the whole of the Mediterranean, from the extreme west (the Balearic Islands and the coast of Catalonia) to the north coast of Africa and, in the east, Syria, Asia Minor and even the Black Sea. There is no doubt, therefore, that the far-ranging activities of

Left: Detail of a sarcophagus found at Sperandio, near Perugia (early fifth century BC; Museo Archeologico, Perugia). The scene shows what may be a whole family travelling with its household goods and cattle. It may have a funerary meaning, but in any case it reflects surprisingly closely what we know from written sources about life in this period.

Below: Attic black-figure amphora (570–550 BC; Museo di Villa Giulia, Rome). The most substantial group of Attic imports consists of this type of so-called 'Tyrrhenian' amphorae, probably used at drinking parties. Scenes from the Greek myths are represented on them.

Etruscan 'pirates' was a matter of some importance in a sea much used by Greeks and Phoenicians as well.

The passage from the hymn to Dionysus (*Homeric Hymns*, VII, 44ff.) about the kidnap also relates an incident at sea:

> And lo the god, within the ship, changed before their eyes into a lion with a fierce and terrifying gaze . . . suddenly it leapt at the captain and seized him; as soon as the sailors saw this they leapt together into the divine sea in order to escape a terrible fate, and they were changed into dolphins. But the god took pity when he saw the helmsman, restrained him and bestowed great happiness upon him.

Further on the members of the crew are identified and characterized; the cruel captain, principally responsible for the kidnapping, is contrasted with the wise old helmsman; and while the captain hoists the sail, the rest of the crew heave on the ropes at each side. The whole ship is described, and there is an extraordinarily striking similarity between this Homeric description and figurative evidence, for a great number of ships were painted or incised on vases within the space of a couple of generations from the middle of the seventh century. These ships are much more elaborate than the small impasto model boats found in Iron Age tombs at Tarquinia, the latter having a flat-bottomed hull with both prow and stern in the shape of a bird's head. Although these models are rather schematic, in some cases we can recognize cargo vessels and in others clearly identifiable warships, with curved hull, high stern with a large closed volute, and a straight prow with a sharp spur below it – the kind of spur which, according to Pliny the Elder, had been invented by an Etruscan. Ships of this kind have certain characteristics already well known to Mycenaean ship builders and adopted by Greek settlers, but some details may be original, such as the metal spur which clearly served the purposes of an aggressive navy.

Etruscan 'pirates' continued to be active over a longer period of history than was once thought and, like the activities in the western Mediterranean of Greeks from the eastern end, their aims were neither political nor expansionist. They were rather to carry on forms of 'commerce' which included piracy as well as trading in raw materials and finished products.

Piracy probably diminished when political institutions gave cities a sense of identity, but no doubt it continued as a form of spontaneous activity, depending on the individual who owned a ship and engaged a crew. It was only in the first half of the sixth century that emporia came into existence, probably subject to rules and regulations imposed by city authorities. Recent excavations at Gravisca, the port for Tarquinia, have shown that Greeks remained on Etruscan soil for a

century from about 580 BC. Merchants were allowed to practise their own religion outside the urban area, and there are many votive inscriptions in Greek which echo the history of Hellenic commerce. At first it was carried on principally by East Greeks, and they were followed, at the end of the sixth century, by a substantial Aeginetan group, led by the famous merchant Sostratos who, according to Herodotus (IV, 152), made a great deal of money out of his trading activities. This may be the time when Etruscan commercial enterprises became subject to controls and therefore suffered a temporary setback, for the diffusion of bucchero around the Mediterranean came to a halt about the middle of the sixth century, and the later distribution of Etruscan objects such as engraved ivories (found at Delos, Rhodes and Cyprus) or the wrought bronzes (found at Athens) which were so highly praised by fifth-century Attic poets, may have been brought about by Greeks who had official trading stations along the Tyrrhenian coast.

At any rate, the defence of their commercial interests in the Tyrrhenian Sea became a practical problem for the Etruscans in the course of the sixth century, to the extent that it necessitated organized fleets. The fragmentary information provided by Greek historians includes mention both of a naval encounter in 580 BC near Lipari in which the Etruscans fought against Rhodes and Cnidus, and of a naval battle about 540 BC in the Sardinian Sea, in which the fleets of Caere (Cerveteri) and its allies the Carthaginians fought the Phocaeans. This is the time when the Carthaginians became the Etruscans' great allies against the Greeks in Sicily. 'The Tyrrhenians and Carthaginians and all those who make treaties are like citizens of a single city,' wrote Aristotle (*Politics*, 1280 a. 36), and there is no doubt that these treaties – which immediately precede

or are of the same period as Rome's treaties with Carthage – show that the city-states of the Tyrrhenian coast exercised some sort of control over navigation and trade.

The defeat of the Carthaginians at Himera (480 BC) and of the Etruscans in a naval battle off Cumae (474 BC) mark the end of Etruscan supremacy in the Tyrrhenian Sea. Commercial activity declined and the Etruscans returned to piracy and harrassment, for which they become proverbial again in the fourth and third centuries, both in Tyrrhenian and Adriatic waters and as far east as the Aegean. By the end of the sixth century, in fact, Etruscan settlers in Emilia had realized that Spina was of vital importance to them, both for maritime and overland trade. This great emporium was inhabited by different ethnic groups (Etruscans, Greeks and Veneti) and was built at the water's edge on rational principles of urban design. Evidence provided by the inhabited area suggests that it was a large commercial city which particularly attracted Greek interest in the fifth century. The merchants of Athens and Corcyra (Corfu) obtained supplies of raw metals and finished metal goods there, as well as animals (especially the famous horses of the Veneti) and amber, which came over the eastern Alps from the Baltic. Local goods such as salt, or finished bronzes from southern Etruria, or Attic pottery direct from Athens, were distributed along the course of the river Po towards the territory of the Ligurians and Celts, and even over the Alpine passes.

The emergence of Spina in the fifth century paralleled the decline of the cities on the Tyrrhenian coast, with the one exception of Populonia. The reason for this exception is that supplies of iron remained fundamental to Tyrrhenian trade, and were certainly of interest to Syracuse in the mid-fifth century, for she sent two military expeditions to the mining area as well as to the west

Right: Inside of a Laconian black-figure cup from Cerveteri (circa 550 BC; Museo Archeologico, Cerveteri). Among imports from Greece was a group of vases manufactured in the workshops of Sparta. This one is attributed to the 'Typhon Painter'.

Left: Via degli Inferi, near Cerveteri. A typical example of the Etruscan technique of rock excavation used to make short cuts for roads.

67

coast of Corsica, where the Etruscans, and Populonia in particular, had set up more than one trading station. It was vital to control the sea between Corsica, Elba and the city of Populonia where the iron was refined, and it is only in the tombs of Populonia and Spina that there are examples of late fifth-century ornate Attic pottery – a style which does not occur anywhere else in Etruria proper.

Only in the second half of the fourth century was there a general revival of trade, and even then it was not to last for long, for Rome began to use its coastal colonies to police the Tyrrhenian coast between Cosa (Ansedonia) and the mouth of the Tiber from the first half of the third century onwards. By then the cities had turned the main focus of their attention to their inland territory, and trade began to be partly regulated by the use of money.

It is vitally important to note that coinage appears in a regular way at Tarquinia, Vetulonia, Populonia, in the Val di Chiana and at Volterra in the closing stages of Etruscan civilization. There were some issues in the mid-sixth century, consisting of bronze ingots with a 'dry twig' sign impressed upon them, and some slightly later gold and silver struck coins, probably from Vulci and Populonia, but their sporadic appearance makes it likely that they were simply private issues, not made by the state authority but by entrepreneurs who used their own seal as a guarantee of the weight and quality of the metal.

At the end of the fourth century, on the other hand, it was the cities themselves which issued bronze and silver coins. Some were cast and others struck (the series of bronze coins from Tarquinia, Volterra and the Val di Chiana were cast, whereas the bronze and silver coins of Populonia and Vetulonia were struck), and they bore the city's name: *Vatl* 'Vetulonia', *Pupluna* or *Pufluna* 'Populonia' and *Velathri* 'Volterra'. Issuing coins became a normal procedure and perhaps also acquired political significance in relations with Rome, for Rome was also beginning to circulate money and had already subjugated certain large Etruscan cities. (Veii, for example, fell in 396 BC.) Coins of a given city-state did not circulate far beyond the territory which was politically subject to it. Those from Vetulonia reached Roselle, those of Populonia circulated all along the coast in the area of Livorno, while those from the Val di Chiana, issued by Arezzo or Chiusi, did not penetrate very far into the territory of Volterra. This money only circulated in the third century – perhaps until the time of the Second Punic War, when there were specially issued coins in the Val di Chiana, possibly intended for the pay of troops sent to help the Roman army against Hannibal.

Cast coins form part of the system of weights based on the Italic *libra*, used in central Italy. The coinage of the coastal cities, on the other hand, had to circulate in places with maritime trade contacts, and recalls Greek money of the Hellenistic Age, even in shape. It is not easy to decide exactly what underlies the first use of money in Etruria, because it has to be realized that even before ordinary legal issues of coinage occurred, the use of weighed quantities of unworked bronze as a means of payment had in itself something of the force of money. State involvement can be seen, therefore, as a means of controlling a trading device whose economic 'value' could be calculated in terms of the weight of the bronze. Only at this stage were the authorities beginning to play a direct part in a trading system which had been operated until then by the most enterprising groups and individuals.

A clear picture of the Etruscan economy at the end of the third century can be obtained from a passage in Livy (XXVIII, 47). When, in 205 BC, the Roman Senate refused Scipio's request to assemble a fleet for an expedition to Africa to distract Hannibal from his devastating military campaigns in Italy, Scipio decided to seek help from those cities which were Rome's allies.

The cities of Etruria were the first to promise to help him, each according to its own resources. Caere promised grain for the sailors and all kinds of provisions, Populonia promised iron, Tarquinia linen for the sails, Volterra grain and wood for making the frames of the ships' hulls, Arezzo three thousand shields and as many helmets, hooked javelins and lances up to a total of fifty thousand of each type of weapon, as well as axes, shovels, sickles, wicker baskets, hand-mills in as great a quantity as could be carried in forty warships, together with one hundred and

Above: Black-figure hydria *from Cerveteri (530–520 BC; Museo Archeologico, Cerveteri). Made in a workshop established at Caere (Cerveteri) around 540 BC by immigrant Phocaean potters. About forty examples of these so-called 'Caeretan' hydriae are known, and most of them have been been found at Cerveteri, although one fragment was discovered at Naucratis, the large Greek emporium on the Nile delta.*

Left: Map of the distribution of bucchero (the shiny black pottery which was in effect Etruscan 'national' pottery in the Archaic period), showing the large volume of trade between 630 and 550 BC. Such trading activities must have been carried on principally by small merchants who owned ships and either transported goods (especially wine) to the south coast of France, or took part in the more extensive eastern Mediterranean trade.

Above: Painting of a cargo ship in a mid fifth-century tomb at Tarquinia, consequently known as the Tomba della Nave.

Right: Attic red-figure stamnos *from Tarquinia (circa 480 BC; Museo Nazionale, Tarquinia). The picture of Europa and the bull was painted by the 'Berlin Painter' — one of the most refined Attic vase-painters working in the 'severe style'. Imports of Attic pottery into Etruria reached their highest point between 530 and 470 BC, and were taken there by famous merchants such as Sostratos, who dedicated to Apollo an inscribed stone anchor found in the area of the Greek sanctuaries at Gravisca, the port of Tarquinia.*

twenty thousand pecks of corn and everything that officers and crew might need for the voyage; Perugia, Chiusi and Roselle offered pine timber for shipbuilding and a large quantity of wheat.

Almost the whole of Etruria, including the coastal cities, seems to be an area producing surpluses in agriculture, textiles and timber. Populonia is the only city still using mineral deposits. Such an impressive quantity of weapons would suggest that Arezzo had a prosperous metal industry, but there is no other evidence for this. Arezzo's contribution is much larger than the other cities', and only in her case are the quantities specified. A possible explanation is that the treaties made between Arezzo and Rome a century earlier, when the Arretine princes needed the help of the Roman army to put down slave revolts, contained clauses which obliged them to make a greater contribution.

Unlike that of Greek cities, Etruscan coinage was not in regular use. At the top of the page is a gold coin from Populonia (Museo Archeologico, Florence), with a lion's head and a sign indicating a value of '50'. It probably dates to the end of the sixth century BC. Below it is a silver coin, also from Populonia (Museo Archeologico, Florence), with a Gorgon's head. It belongs to a series current in the fourth and third centuries. At that period it was the state authorities themselves who issued coins, including on them the name of the city: Pupluna in this case.

71

The Etruscan Language

Classical authors are unanimous in attributing to the Greeks the introduction of alphabetical writing into Italy. Tacitus in particular (*Annals*, XI, 14) reports that 'writing in Italy was taught to the Etruscans by Demaratus of Corinth and to the Aborigines (the ancestors of the Latins) by Evander of Arcadia'. Since Demaratus appears to have settled at Tarquinia (see page 64) about the middle of the seventh century, the first Etruscan inscriptions ought to date from that time. In fact they appear about fifty years earlier, around 700 BC, and reveal a system of writing adapted from a model which can be identified as the Greek alphabet of the Euboean settlers. At an initial stage, this adaptation involved dropping certain Greek letters (*beta* and *delta*, which represented the sounds *b* and *d* in Greek, and *omicron*, which represented the sound *o*), and later on, during the seventh century, the group of letters *digamma*-plus-aspirate was added to indicate the sound *f*, and a letter based on *sade*, as used in Corinthian writing, to represent a variant of the sound *s*.

What happened is perfectly understandable if it is related to the more general problem of the difficulties which arise when a system of writing created to deal with the sounds of one language is adapted to the needs of another. The dropping of certain letters (the fact that *omicron, beta* and *delta* are not used shows that the opposition between the velar vowels *o* and *u* and between voiced and unvoiced consonants was not appreciable in Etruscan) and the adding of others (for example, the use of *sade* to indicate a different quality of sibilant from that already represented by *sigma*) show that the Etruscan

Urn lid from Volterra (late second century BC; Museo Guarnacci, Volterra). The dead man is half reclining and holds an open diptych in his right hand.

73

Transcription	a	c	e	v	z	h	θ	i	k	l	m	n	p	ś	q	r	s̃s	t	u	φ	χ
Ischia Cuma	A	⟨	⤳	⤳	I	⧖	⊕	I	Ж	⤳	⋔	⋔	⌐		⟡	⟢	⟩⟩	T	Y	Φ	Ψ
Etruria	A	⊃	⤳	⤳	I	⧖	⊗	I	Ж	⤳	M	M	⌐	M	⟡	⟢	⟩⟩	T	Y	Φ	Ψ

phonetic system was considerably different from that of Greek. This difference was 'felt' by those who were responsible for devising an alphabetical system for Etruscan – that is to say, by the Etruscans who knew spoken and written Greek and, similarly, by the Greeks who knew Etruscan before it had an alphabet.

Apart from certain variants used in writing to distinguish between certain sounds (velars and the two sibilants), Etruscan writing came to adopt a single system and throughout its life continued to be set down from right to left, as was the Euboean alphabet from which it originated and which came to Etruria in the early seventh century.

Before embarking on the central theme of this chapter, it will be as well to deal first with one basic problem about the Etruscans. The language which we find in inscriptions dating from the seventh to the first century BC is not Indo-European, and has a regular phonetic and morphological system which, as happens with any spoken idiom, changes somewhat in the course of time. The available writings are not particularly abundant (about 10,000 texts) and are largely confined to funerary inscriptions indicating no more than the names of the dead. Hence the impossibility of dealing satisfactorily with the relationship between Etruscan and the other ancient languages.

Successive scholars have tried to solve this problem by comparing Etruscan with other non-Indo-European languages for which we have equally insufficient textual evidence, and they have all failed. As has recently been confirmed, the only possible comparison on a historical basis seems to be with a language for which we have one single inscription in a western Greek alphabet. This is a late sixth-century inscription discovered on the island of Lemnos in the northern Aegean, and although its letters are different from those of the Etruscan alphabet, which belongs to the separate Euboean tradition, there are surprising linguistic affinities between the two. Some similarities appear in the phonetic system. There is the same lack of distinction between voiced and unvoiced consonants, one of the velar vowels is missing (Etruscan, as we have seen, only uses *u*, whereas Lemnian only uses *o*), and there are two sibilants. As regards morphology, we find similar formulae for indicating age and dates, and as

regards lexis, we find that names are of the same type and that numerals indicating tens are formed in the same way. In other words, it looks as though Lemnian and Etruscan derive from a common source, but by the time written evidence of its existence is available, it has become so diversified that these two forms, spoken in widely different places and without any contact between them, have taken on their own individual characteristics. This is a quite different situation from that, let us say, of twelfth-century AD Provençal and Italian texts, of which it could never be said that they are forms of a single language which was originally Latin. It is also interesting to note that the inhabitants of Lemnos, where Athens established a colony in the early fifth century, are called Tyrrhenians by Greek writers – the same name that they gave the Etruscans. These linguistic facts suggest a relationship between Lemnian and Etruscan which one might expect to be a reflection, historically speaking, of some kind of affinity between the two peoples. Such an affinity, however, would have its roots deep in the mythical times of prehistory, in the closing centuries of the second millenium BC, an era to which Herodotus attributed 'stories' he had gathered from the historiographical traditions of Ionia (in the Near East), and to which he dated the migration to Tuscany of the Lydians led by Tyrrhenus. On the other hand, another Greek historian, Anticlides, writing in the third century BC, attributed the colonization of Lemnos and Imbros, and the subsequent occupation of Italian soil, to another mythical people, the Pelasgians – led, once again, by Tyrrhenus.

This tenuous linguistic link is all that exists to suggest that, in spite of its legendary trappings, there might be some truth in the famous theory of the eastern origins of the Etruscans. By the time their culture takes its place in the history of ancient Italy, their language, as seen in seventh-century inscriptions, seems to have been at home in Italy for some time, especially if one looks at the many loan words. Among the names of persons, for example, Etruscan had by then taken over many Italic forms: *Mamarce, Kavie, Thifarie, Kaisie, Metie* and *Numesie*, which correspond to Latin *Mamercus, Gavius, Tiberius, Caesius, Mettius* and *Numerius*. And among the few common nouns which have come down to us, *spanti* ('plate') comes from Umbrian.

Borrowed words from Greek come later. They can be dated to the time when the Etruscans came into contact with Greek settlers and, at the earliest stage, are mostly common nouns, especially names of vases (see page 55). (At this period almost all Etruscan inscriptions are on pottery.) As previously shown in connection with the words for wine and oil or for instruments such as the *groma*, it is clear that the 'civilizing' influence of the Greeks involved the introduction into Etruscan culture of objects which did not exist locally and which

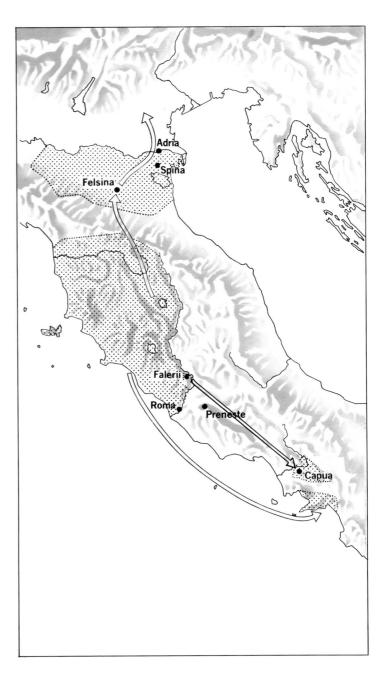

Above: The Etruscans introduced writing to other peoples of ancient Italy, whose languages were Indo-European. There are fifth-century inscriptions from Capua in Oscan (an Italic language), which use the same kind of writing as Etruscan. The alphabet used in the Veneto at the same period was a slightly modified version of that provided by the Etruscans living in the inland areas of northern Italy.

Left: This strangely shaped little bucchero vase (perhaps an inkwell?) has on its body an exercise in syllabic writing, and on its base a whole alphabet derived from that of Greek. The vase comes from a 'princely' tomb at Cerveteri (mid-seventh century BC; Musei Vaticani).

were therefore taken over complete with their names. Greek personal names, on the other hand, had much less influence. This may be because the corpus of Etruscan names had already absorbed certain Italic elements and had become fixed during the seventh century, so that Greek proper names were not able to penetrate local culture. There are, it is true, some cases of 'naturalization' in the seventh century, as one can tell from inscriptions. Whereas Demaratus (page 64) gave his own children Etruscan names, some Greek craftsmen and merchants must have kept their original names when they settled into Etruscan communities. A *Teleklés* and a *Hippokrátes*, for example, etruscanize their names into *Telicle* and *Hipucrate*. Generally such exceptions had no subsequent influence, however, save for the case of some slaves of Greek origin who came to Etruria in the second century to work on the land.

Etruscan writing as it has come down to us goes back earlier than any of the other languages which existed in ancient Italy (for example, Latin, originally spoken only in *Latium vetus*; Faliscan, spoken in the territory of Falerii; the Sabellic languages, spoken in Sabina and other parts of central and southern Italy; and Venetic, spoken in the Veneto). This fact bears witness to the historical and commercial importance of Etruria in relation to the Greek world. In the history of writing and its diffusion in Italy, Etruria had in its turn a very important 'civilizing' role to play.

Generally speaking, the writing systems in use in Latium in the seventh century seem to develop in their own way and in accordance with their own linguistic diversity, although one can clearly see that they derive from Etruscan and maintain a reciprocal relationship with it. In spite of their differences, Latin and Faliscan both preserve certain letters of the Greek alphabet in order to represent sounds similar to those in Greek (Latin keeps *omicron, beta* and *delta*; Faliscan keeps *delta* and *omicron*), but they do not use certain Greek letters (the aspirates) which the Etruscans had used. On the other hand, there are similarities in the way they write the other letters, which look as though they had been written by an Etruscan from Cerveteri or Veii.

There are just a few sixth-century inscriptions from Sabina, Abruzzo and Campania to provide us with evidence of 'Italic' writing, which adopts a quite different, not to say contrary system to that of Etruria and Latium. Fifth-century Oscan inscriptions found near Capua, on the other hand, use a system which clearly derives from Etruscan, as do both the few Umbrian inscriptions from before the third century, and fifth-century Venetic inscriptions. The consequences of all this for our understanding of Etruscan cultural history are quite clear. Wherever the Etruscans exert a predominating cultural influence, they provide the local population with a means of written communication

Above: Inscribed vase dedication from the sanctuary outside Veii (580–560 BC; Museo di Villa Giulia, Rome). The text is fairly clear: 'Mamarce Apunie *dedicated me to Vena'*.

Left: This strangely shaped bucchero object may be an incense holder. The stem bears the craftsman's signature ('I was made by Larthuza Kulenie'), *perhaps because he was conscious of his own special skill. It comes from a tomb at Artimino, near Florence (late seventh century* BC; *Museo Archeologico, Florence).*

and record-keeping. Both the Campanians and the Veneti adopted this system of writing under direct pressure from southern and northern Etruscans, who had respectively colonized Capua and the Po valley.

The Literate Classes

The introduction of the alphabet into Tuscany and Latium can be seen as just one of the results of a much broader process of cultural change. For the region which receives the alphabet, writing is an innovation forming part of a whole series of transformations in various areas of culture; and archaeological evidence, as we have seen, places these occurrences towards the end of the eighth century. The acceptance and subsequent modification of the Euboean Greek alphabet signifies learning a method of recording certain matters mostly concerned with trading activities, exactly as

had happened in the case of the Greek alphabet in the ninth century in the emporia on the Phoenician coast. The spread of writing in eighth-century Greece, on the other hand, can be seen as something closely linked to the coming into being of cities. It is the means of disseminating a culture whose sphere of influence is the city. Inscriptions in Etruria dating to the first half of the seventh century, however, include some in the culturally most significant tombs. For the most part they are found on luxury objects preserved beside the dead body in 'princely' tombs, and the inscription is a sort of added confirmation of the importance of the object in itself. Thus the texts invariably supply the name of the owner of the object and sometimes also the name of the person from whom it was a gift (see page 63), thereby confirming that writing was current amongst the higher social classes.

More information as to the élite nature of writing in the seventh century can be obtained from objects bearing the alphabet itself, since they are by their nature connected with the practice of writing. One such object is the famous tablet from Marsiliana d'Albegna, found in a 'princely' tomb together with the stylus and eraser used in writing. In one of the rich burials of the Regolini-Galassi tomb at Cerveteri there is a sort of bucchero inkwell with the alphabet engraved on it, together with a whole syllabary. There is also a small bucchero amphora from the monumental tomb at Monte Aguzzo near Formello (Veii), on which the alphabet appears as part of a sort of syllabic game, followed by a text containing the basic facts about the amphora: 'I . . . of Atianai. Given to Venel. Velthur made me.' The alphabet could be written out for various reasons, but when engraved on objects which are symbolically connected with the actual practice of writing, it acquires a special significance. It may also identify the circumstances in which knowledge of the alphabet becomes a matter of specific social distinction, especially if that knowledge is set out in written form. It can then be used to indicate the owner of an object and to record the name of the person who gave it. Hence one can say that, since writing reached Etruria when different social classes had already appeared there, and when wealth seems already to have been concentrated in the hands of a small aristocracy, it can be seen as a cultural element existing initially at higher social levels.

In the second half of the seventh century, writing spread more rapidly. If we were to judge solely by the texts which we now possess, the picture we would have of the spread of writing in Tuscany and Latium would be extraordinary, for there is a strong concentration of inscriptions in Etruscan territory and very few in Latium, in spite of the fact that Latium has whole cemeteries where, until the end of the century, the social situation and distribution of wealth are similar to

Etruria. If we move out of Latium, the incidence of inscriptions decreases still further, even in Greek settlements in Campania. It is difficult to imagine that the Etruscans used writing at a time when it was not in use in Italy among Latins and Greeks as well. The explanation must be that it is precisely the social value of writing, as something prestigious to be shown off, which accounts for the high incidence (approximately a hundred) of Etruscan written texts of the seventh century.

The large number of inscriptions appearing toward the end of the century, however, and their distribution across Etruscan territory, can be explained as part of a whole range of cultural innovations connected with the development of an urban society, in which a flourishing group of craftsmen acted as agents for transmitting culture. In other words, the use of writing and the teaching of the alphabet were no longer confined to the ruling class of aristocratic families. Indeed the teaching of the

Above: Relief on an urn from Volterra (end of the second century BC; Museo Guarnacci, Volterra), showing a scene in school or at a public reading. The figures are reading and commenting on volumina, *which they hold open, bearing witness to the importance of written documents.*

Right: Fragments of the inscribed elogium *of* Velthur Spurinna. *This historical character lived at Tarquinia in the closing decades of the fifth century BC (Museo Nazionale, Tarquinia).*

alphabet probably also moved into schools set up for this purpose, perhaps at sanctuaries.

During this period of urban culture, however, the spread of writing is closely related to its use for 'public' purposes. It becomes a vital adjunct of political life, and in this area the scribes appear to have played a fundamentally important role. Among the acts of heroism reported by Roman historians in the wars against Porsenna at the end of the sixth century, there is the famous episode of Mucius Scaevola, who managed to make his way into the Etruscan camp just at the moment when the soldiers were receiving their pay.

> The scribe was sitting next to the king, wearing very similar clothes to his, and was very busy as all the soldiers sought his attention; Scaevola dared not ask which of the two was Porsenna for fear that his ignorance would give him away, and he killed the scribe, mistaking him for the king (*Livy*, II, 12).

The story has something of the flavour of legend, it is true, but it has been observed that there are some early fifth-century *cippi* from Chiusi with relief decoration in which the figure of a scribe, dressed in tunic and cloak, appears twice. In one scene he is on the judges' platform at an athletics competition, and in another he appears to be writing down on a tablet something which is dictated by another figure who sits holding a small sceptre.

It appears that scribes took part in official ceremonies in order to write down what was necessary, and the tablets evidently remained in the archives for as long as was thought useful. Scribes were vitally important as secretaries. Among the entourage of magistrates represented in reliefs on Hellenistic sarcophagi and tombs, only the scribe, armed with one large tablet or a pile of small ones, is near the magistrate himself, while musicians and lictors lead the procession.

While the scribe's task was to record occasional events in which a magistrate was directly involved, it must have been priests who were responsible for recording more important events. In Rome, for example, the priests recorded year by year, in the form of a brief chronicle, all the important political events, under the names of the magistrates then in office. In the mid-sixth century, priests in Etruria had evolved a system of 'learned' writing at the sanctuaries in which the chain of writing is no longer continuous. Instead of all the words being run together, they are punctuated with one, two or three points, placed (the rules are not always very strict, however) after a closed syllable, that is to say one which does not consist of a consonant-plus-vowel group. The evidence we have for this system is found on an object which comes directly from a priestly source. This is an inscription, engraved before firing, on an early fifth-century terracotta tile found at S.

Maria Capua Vetere and now in the East Berlin archaeological museum. The text is a long ritual, listing prescribed sacrifices to the deities of the underworld, and cannot be 'translated' in all its details. As one would expect in a text of this kind, the formulae used are brief and frequently repeated, while the technical language is very precise and full of nuances of meaning. The words used to convey the sacrificial act, for example, are *tule, ilucve, apirase* and *acalu*, and they are used singly or in groups, depending on the gods concerned. The types of offering also vary: *vacil* refers to a general offering, but there are also *itna, zusle, tartiria, turza* and *zizriin puiia*. The text is also conceived as something 'literary'. It is intentionally divided into chapters with dividing lines to indicate new paragraphs, and clearly ends with the signature of the person who 'composed' or actually wrote it: . . . *uris zichunce* ('uris wrote'). This signature confirms the importance of the scribe, or perhaps we should call him transcriber if we think of him as a man whose job was to set down the prescriptions for private or public rites.

The existence of such a long religious text makes it quite certain that there must have been other written documents setting out regulations of a public kind, such as would be essential in a society dominated by an aristocracy. It is no coincidence that it was about the mid-fifth century that the regulations known as the 'Law of the XII Tables' were set down in writing in Rome; and according to Livy they were 'the source of all private and public law'. An example of public regulations in which writing has its part to play can be found in the Crocifisso del Tufo cemetery at Orvieto (see page 18). The tombs are arranged to occupy an equal area and each one bears a more or less identical inscription indicating the owner. This would appear to have been made obligatory by the state in order to ensure that each individual enjoyed his rights of ownership; and indeed in a few cases the inscriptions have been erased and new ones referring to different individuals put in their place.

Direct evidence of the increasing use of writing is unfortunately lacking, but one can see its effect on the Etruscan view of life after death. Once writing has become widespread, the book, in the form of a *volumen* or roll, also becomes an attribute of the funerary gods, who unroll it to reveal man's destiny in written form. There is a late fifth-century sarcophagus lid from Chianciano on which a winged female figure, beside the dead man, is unrolling one of these books. This is one of the earliest pieces of evidence as to the nature of Etruscan religion, which was partly based, as we shall see, on revealed truths transmitted in written form.

In the private sphere, the number of inscriptions indicating possession decreases in the fifth century, and those indicating gifts cease altogether after about 550

BC. Hence we can conclude that the practice had been slowly dying out. Instead, inscriptions seem to become very frequent on objects designed for special uses, such as vases, gems for rings, or bronze mirrors, where the scenes depicted often have 'captions' beside the different characters to assist in identifying the subjects and episodes represented. This custom comes straight from Greek pottery, which was imported in large quantities in the sixth and fifth centuries. Hence one finds that it is the gods and heroes of Greece in some of the most characteristic episodes of their legends who appear on objects made in Etruria. Here they represent a 'pleasure-seeking' lay culture, and in pictorial form they also help to record and preserve legends and stories. The most frequently written names are those of Heracles (*Hercle*), Achilles (*Achle*), Ulysses (*Uturze*), the Seven against Thebes, Helen and Menelaus. These provide indirect evidence of the popularity enjoyed by Greek legends in Etruria at that time, for they were no longer passed on solely by word of mouth, as in Archaic times, but also by pictures – and perhaps by the written word as well.

Literature

In the fourth century, when scenes of the kind just mentioned are most frequently found, the Etruscans were seen by the Romans as a people whose culture was worth learning about. Towards the middle of the fourth century, boys from the Roman *nobilitas* were educated in Etruria. Livy reports (IX, 36, 3) that Marcus, one of the Fabii, was educated at Caere. 'He knew Etruscan writings and could speak Etruscan well. I have evidence that in those days boys were taught Etruscan just as they are now taught Greek.'

There is a famous incident depicted in the Tomba François at Vulci (the paintings from which are now in the Villa Albani in Rome), involving historical characters known from written sources, and painted shortly after the mid-fourth century BC. The above detail shows Macstrna *(Servius Tullius) on the left, in the act of freeing Caelius Vibenna, a military leader from Vulci. Behind him are three pairs of duellers, each of whom is identified by name, those who are enemies having their ethnic origin indicated as well. Written sources do not mention this particular episode, but they do speak of the alliance between Mastarna-Servius Tullius and the brothers Aulus and Caelius Vibenna of Vulci, who came to Rome during the reign of Tarquinius Priscus.*

There is no doubt that it was in the second century that literacy became most widespread in Etruria. In northern Etruria, the cemeteries in the Chiusi and Perugia areas have provided us with about five thousand written inscriptions on funerary objects, some of which belonged to people of quite lowly condition: the *lautni* referred to earlier. Many members of the 'middle class' of Volterra – but only males – are depicted on urn lids with sets of writing tablets in their hands. Sometimes the tablets are held open, in which case the name of the dead person is inscribed on them. Sometimes the men concerned hold an open roll which to all intents and purposes constitutes a *volumen* or 'book'.

Literacy, then, had a definite cultural value, and its representation in symbolic terms on funerary urns could serve partly to indicate the dead person's position in life. Waxed tablets, on which one wrote with a pointed stylus, were useful for education, trade, keeping records and so on, whereas the 'book' or *volumen* was less impermanent in that what was written on it could be preserved. Books were widely used in Hellenistic times, to the extent that there grew up what one might reasonably describe as a publishing system. In Italy, the first books were made of linen, but then the use of writing must also have been spread through the use of papyrus (which came direct from Alexandria). And then there was parchment, obtained by means of techniques developed primarily in the kingdom of Pergamon at the beginning of the second century. The wars of conquest in Greece, moreover, allowed Roman generals to bring back to Rome a larger quantity of books as well as works of art. Paulus Emilius, the victor at the battle of Pydna in 168 BC, chose as his part of the booty the library of King Perseus of Macedonia.

The text painted or engraved on the representations of *volumina* held open before us on urn and sarcophagus lids naturally tell of the dead person's life. There is a sarcophagus of about 180 BC from Tarquinia, on which the *volumen* bears one of the longest funerary inscriptions we know. It begins: 'Laris Pulena son of Larce, grandson of Larth, great-grandson of Velthur, descendant(?) of the Greek Laris Pule. It was he who composed this book on haruspicy(?) and who in the city of Tarquinia . . .'. The rest of the text is much less easy to understand, but the beginning lists the dead man's ancestors, who, he claims, are of Greek origin, and he also claims the distinction of having written a book on haruspicy, the science concerned with divination from the inspection of animal entrails.

The eulogistic tone of these funerary inscriptions is also found in those of the great Roman families of the third and second century, who used them to extol achievements which, in a Rome which was dominated by the aristocracy, were usually of a personal or family nature. It seems likely that the 'historical' content of this type of inscription, with its concern to establish ancestry, depended not merely on an oral tradition, but also on a written one, as preserved in family archives. This is the only possible explanation for the Latin epitaphs below the statues of some Etruscans of the Spurinna family in the temple of *Iuno Regina* at Tarquinia, for they lived several centuries before the time of the Emperor Claudius, when the epitaphs were engraved. These epitaphs provide a description of the most important political achievements of the persons concerned in the usual terse style of inscriptions.

> Velthur Spurinna, son of Larth, was twice made praetor. While a magistrate he commanded an army in Sicily and took another there. He was the first of all the Etruscans to cross the sea with an armed force(?), from whom he received a shield and a gold crown in recognition of his distinction.

> Aulus Spurinna, son of Velthur, was made praetor three times. He deposed Orgolnius Velturnense(?) king of the Caeretans. He liberated Arezzo when it was in the throes of a slave war. He captured(?) nine citadels from the Latins. . . .

In spite of gaps in the texts, it seems clear that the father and son concerned had been magistrates at Tarquinia. The father was probably the man who commanded a military force sent to the assistance of Athens in Sicily in 413 BC in three fifty-oared ships (*Thucydides*, VI, 103). The son, on the other hand, was involved in a series of local political conflicts, probably dating to just before the middle of the fourth century, in which Rome and its allies the Latins also played a part.

It may be that the father, Velthur Spurinna, can be identified as the owner of the famous painted Tomba dell'Orco I at Tarquinia, with its long eulogy in Etruscan containing information similar to the above. It seems likely that, in addition to family archives, there were also compilations of a more literary kind in the form of 'family histories', and these may have provided information for the eulogies of the two Spurinnas. We know that such histories existed in late Republican times, and they belong to a literary genre which enjoyed a considerable success in Rome in the first century BC. This was antiquarian literature, whose purpose was to trace the history and traditions of the people of ancient Italy. The greatest exponent of the genre was Varro (116–27 BC), and his interest in the Etruscans is clear from a few fragments and some of the few works of his to survive (few, that is, relative to his vast output in many different fields). It is likely that one of his sources of information was the *Tuscae historiae* – writings which collected together Etruscan traditions and arranged them according to their *saecula*, the periods into which the Etruscans divided their history. These writings may also have been used by the most important scholars of early Imperial times who were interested in the Etruscans, such as Verrius Flaccus, author of *Rerum etruscarum libri*, and the Emperor Claudius himself, who wrote twenty volumes of *Tyrrhenica*. These books have been lost, though there are brief references to them in later works, but their loss is partially compensated for by a passage in a speech by Claudius in which specific reference is made to 'Etruscan writers':

> Between Tarquinius Priscus and his son or grandson (Tarquin the Proud) – the sources do not agree on this point – must be placed Servius Tullius. According to Latin writers, his mother was the slave Ocresia; according to Etruscan writers, he was a close friend of Caelius Vibenna and was involved in all the latter's adventures. After a series of events, he went to Etruria with

the remainder of Caelius's troops, and occupied Mons Caelius, which he named after his general; and, having changed his name to Servius Tullius (he was called Mastarna in Etruscan), he held sway there to the immense benefit of the state. (CIL, XIII, 1968, I, 17ff.)

There is an echo of this tradition in a late commentator who probably got his information from Verrius Flaccus. According to a certain tradition, the *Vicus Tuscus* or 'Etruscan quarter' in Rome was so called because 'this was where there dwelt the brothers Caelius and Aulus Vibenna, who went to Rome, so we are told, together with Mastarna in the train of King Tarquin' (*Festus*, 486 L).

The Etruscans thus had their own tradition of historical writing, which must, incidentally, have provided a rather different version from Roman annals of the origins and achievements of Servius Tullius, the sixth king of Rome, who was thought to have been responsible, as we have seen, for the definitive establishment of Rome as a city. A very interesting light is thrown on the same events by paintings in the François Tomb at Vulci, dating to the second half of the fourth century. Three pairs of duellers are shown along one wall, and in one corner a naked man, whose name is given as *Macstrna*, is in the act of freeing another man, *Caile Vipinas*, from his chains. Three of the duellers can be seen to be suffering defeat, each being given his name and the place of origin of his people (Volsinii, Sovanna and perhaps Falerii). Amongst the three victors the name of *Avile Vipinas* stands out. Another duel is depicted separately, showing a certain *Marce Camitlnas* in the act of running through a Roman named *Cneve Turchunies*. One almost has the impression of watching a war in which generals and soldiers – presumably from Vulci – are fighting against men from Rome and the cities of the Tiber valley. The dramatic climax of the scene is the freeing of Caelius Vibenna by Mastarna (Servius Tullius). It may be that these scenes depict one of those events which, according to the Emperor Claudius, preceded the arrival of the Vibennas and Mastarna in Rome.

Another literary genre which enjoyed much greater success in the first century BC and which was based on writings composed earlier in Etruria, was that concerned with religious knowledge, known as the *disciplina etrusca*. The Roman Senate may have been responsible for seeing that all the religious lore which had been accumulated in Etruria through the ages should be collected together. Cicero himself tells us what was in these books, for he divides them by content into *libri fulgurales* on the interpretation of lightning, *libri haruspicini* on the interpretation of animal entrails, and *libri rituales* on the rites to be used on various public occasions.

*Above: Another detail of the fresco from the Tomba François at Vulci, showing the figure of Caelius Vibenna (*Caile Vipinas *in Etruscan). In a state of heroic nudity, he is being freed from his chains by Mastarna.*

Left: Etrusco-Corinthian krater *with a scene of sacrifice from Cerveteri (580–560 BC; Museo Archeologico, Cerveteri). A knowledge of Greek stories and myths was fundamental to Etruscan oral – and perhaps written – culture. Such themes occur very frequently in Etruscan figurative art from the end of the seventh century BC.*

In troubled times of first-century BC civil strife in Rome, it seems almost that culture turned largely to ancient forms of belief, as though they might lend new life to an enfeebled religious tradition, and restore to official religion those forms of superstition which involved a specifically Etruscan view of nature and the world. Hence the appearance of popular religious works in Latin by authors of Etruscan origin now living in Rome. In the first half of the first century BC, Lucius Tarquitius Priscus apparently translated what had been set down on the subject of the *disciplina etrusca*. His books were still in circulation as *Tarquitiani* in the fourth century AD, and they provided a valuable source for later scholars. Pliny the Elder used them for Books II and XI of his *Natural History*, and Macrobius used them to illustrate certain remedies against unfavourable omens in the vegetable kingdom. Aulus Caecina of Volterra, a friend and correspondent of Cicero who became involved in politics by writing a pamphlet attacking Julius Caesar, was also a well-known popularizer of the *disciplina etrusca* in Rome, to the extent that his writings became Seneca's main source for his *Naturales Quaestiones*. Evidence such as the Laris Pulena inscription which speaks of a 'book on haruspicy' suggests that Etruscan literature was primarily concerned with religion, and, at the end of the second century BC, the Greek philosopher Posidonius confirmed that the Etruscans had cultivated literature, especially the natural and religious sciences – largely to the exclusion of literary genres intended for pleasure.

This, however, runs counter to what Varro tells us about a certain Volnius, who may have lived at the end of the second century BC, and who had apparently written tragedies in Etruscan; and it also contrasts with the extensive knowledge of myths from Greek tragedies which we find represented in second-century urn reliefs from Chiusi and Volterra. These are funerary objects belonging to an élite who seem to have had a predilection for certain themes, such as the Trojan cycle of the Seven against Thebes, and the stories of Orestes – all themes used by Latin tragedians of the third and second centuries BC, such as Livius Andronicus, Naevius, Ennius, Pacuvius and Accius.

As in the case of Roman literature, so that of the Etruscans depended on the most important traditions of a family kind. It is true that religious literature had priestly sources, but, as we shall see, its true origin was claimed by the 'princes' who were supposed to have written down the precepts dictated to them by the mythical Tages. Historical literature, moreover, was based on family traditions preserved by means of special records kept in archives or in proper family trees kept in homes. And 'lay' literature, that is, literature for pleasure, may also in a sense have acquired its own written tradition, in Etruria as in Rome, once Hellenistic culture had reached those Etruscan cities where a local tradition already thrived.

As in Rome before the wars against Taranto, which brought the *nobilitas* into direct contact with the poets of *Magna Graecia*, so in Etruria too, written forms of culture must have been limited to texts of a public kind; whereas most forms of culture for entertainment, such as poetry recited at banquets, or lullabies, or funeral laments, must have formed part of an oral tradition. The only Etruscan literary text we have is a religious one, demonstrating how the written word was used as a means of recording a branch of learning which was jealously preserved from generation to generation. The text in question is the famous linen book now in the museum at Zagreb. No one knows how it was discovered. About 1848, a Croatian collector by the name of Mihajlo Barić apparently bought some Egyptian antiquities either during a trip to Egypt or perhaps from a New York antiquarian. When the collection came into the possession of the Jugoslav Academy in Zagreb in 1867, the book had been split up into separate strips which were used as binding for a mummy. Although there is no evidence to support it, the claim has also been made that the bindings had been used on the mummy of a female child in the same collection. Twenty-five years were to pass before J. Krall gave official recognition, in 1892, to the fact that the bindings were part of the longest known Etruscan text. The linen of which the book is made had been split into a number of different strips, between 6 and 7 centimetres (about 2.5 inches) wide; and it has been possible to reassemble just over 13.5 metres (45 feet) of the book, to a width of more than 33 centimetres (13 inches). As in the case of ancient books generally, it must have been rolled up. The text is written in red ink in twelve columns of about thirty lines each, the columns being divided by vertical lines, and the book has to be unrolled from right to left, since that is how the writing reads.

The text contains more than twelve hundred words and is probably divided into paragraphs, each of which describes the religious ceremonies to be carried out on certain days of the year. These instructions often remain unchanged, with variations solely in the names of the gods, while offerings of wine and animals depend on the advantages to be gained by a city (unidentified) or by the Etruscan nation as a whole. The fact that the book contains liturgical formulae means that these are often repeated, and one notices as a result that there are many variations in spelling, due to the inexperience of the scribe, who may have written the book from dictation.

Hence we see that this text recorded ceremonies held in an Etruscan community, perhaps situated in the central or upper Nile valley well into the first century BC. This is not so surprising if we recall that another group of Etruscans, led by a certain *Marce Unata* (perhaps from Chiusi), had settled in Tunisia at the same period, occupying land in the valley of the Ouhed Miliane, which flows into the sea near Carthage. They had carried out the appropriate rites for marking out their land under the protection of *Tinia*, in accordance with customs handed down from generation to generation in their homeland.

This is another case of the written word leaving its country of origin and living out the final stages of a culture which was now being completely swept away in the process of romanization.

Caeretan hydria *(530–520* BC*; Museo di Villa Giulia, Rome). One of the characters from Greek mythology who appears in Etruscan figurative art is Heracles. This version of one of the twelve labours imposed on him by Eurystheus has a humorous element. Heracles arrives from Hades with Cerberus, and Eurystheus in his fright takes refuge in a* pithos.

Spiritual and Religious Life

It is a well-known fact that if you want to understand the religious life of a particular people, the best way to go about it is to gather together as many oral and written texts as possible, until you have sufficient to enable you to interpret the data they provide. In the case of a past civilization such as that of the Etruscans, which has left us very few texts – and those that we have are written in a language which is difficult to understand – Greek and Latin sources can act as intermediaries. Any intermediary, however, is himself an interpreter in that he sees what he tells us about from his own particular point of view, and that is itself related to the attitudes of his own times. Hence it is by no means easy to get to the bottom of matters concerning the religious life of the Etruscans by referring to Latin writers, because, from Cicero onwards, their view of the situation is inevitably that of the age in which they lived.

A different kind of approach is to study examples of the figurative arts in which myths or gods are represented. But this kind of evidence also needs corroboration, because it is indirect in the sense that it presents the symbols of a psychological reality for which it is difficult to provide a historical reconstruction without running the risk of ending up with some of the varied and incredible fictions which have indeed been produced in the past.

The Etruscans are presented in Latin literature as having a wide variety of superstitions and religious practices, and they had built up a substantial body of learning in divination which, as has already been

Silver gilt vessel from Chiusi (circa 650 BC; Museo Archeologico, Florence). This is one of the earliest known illustrations of a sacrificial ceremony. Warriors and horsemen are involved, as well as the bearers of the sacrificial sheep and pigs.

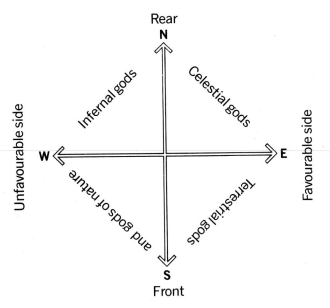

Rear
N

Infernal gods

Celestial gods

Unfavourable side

W

E

Favourable side

and gods of nature

Terrestrial gods

S
Front

The division of the heavens

pointed out, had its own literature. It was the Emperor Claudius, with his well-known mania for etruscology, who was chiefly responsible for gathering Etruscan learning on the interpretation of natural phenomena.

It often happened that when the State fell upon evil days, the Etruscan soothsayers were summoned to Rome and ceremonies were revived and thereafter faithfully observed. The leading citizens of Etruria, either of their own accord or at the request of the Roman Senate, were the depositaries of this religious learning and passed it on to their descendants (Tacitus, *Annals*, XI, 15).

The above is part of the speech which Claudius made to the Senate in a successful attempt to convince them that they should entrust to the *pontifices* – the highest religious authority in the Roman state – the task of reorganizing haruspicy and the college of sixty *haruspices* who were responsible for it.

Haruspicy took different forms at different times, and we now have only a few fragments from first-century Etruscan writers mentioned earlier (Aulus Caecina, Nigidius Figulus and Tarquitius Priscus), but many later Roman writers have told us something of the contents of their books, deriving their information either directly from Etruscan sources or from translations of first-century texts. Thus, in his *Naturales Quaestiones*, Seneca makes direct use of Aulus Caecina's *Disciplina Etrusca*; Pliny the Elder's *Natural History* makes direct use of Tarquitius Priscus's collection of Etruscan prodigies. One of those most interested in Etruscan culture was Verrius Flaccus, who may have made direct use of texts in Etruscan, as may also a certain Cornelius Labeo, a writer of the second century AD who is supposed to have written a commentary on Etruscan religion in fifteen volumes.

Roman writers in particular stress the fundamental importance of written texts in the religious practices of the Etruscans, since their entire religious tradition was set down there. And since these writings were attributed in the first place to mythical characters such as Tages or the nymph Vegoia, mentioned earlier, the Etruscan religion was to all intents and purposes a revealed religion, the substance of which was handed down in sacred books, as in the case of modern religions.

In his book *On Divination*, for example, Cicero tells a very significant story about one of the practices which formed part of Etruscan divinatory learning, namely the examination and interpretation of animal livers.

The story is told that while the fields near Tarquinia were being ploughed, there suddenly leaped forth from a more deeply ploughed furrow a certain Tages, who spoke to the plough-man. The Etruscan books say that Tages had the appearance of a child but the wisdom of an old man. The peasant was taken aback at the sight of him and gave a cry of amazement; people gathered and soon it seemed almost as if the whole of Etruria was gathered in that spot. Tages then spoke on many subjects to the listen-ing crowd, and they collected and wrote down everything he said. What he said was in fact the science of haruspicy which, as time passed, gathered other ideas, all of which were based on the principle laid down by Tages (*On Divination*, II, 23).

The child disappeared as suddenly as he had appeared. But the truths which he revealed were passed down in written form, and could therefore only be understood by those who could read. Other Latin writers report that it was the ancient kings known as *lucumones* who transcribed the revelations, or that the god himself dictated them to twelve sons of the Etruscan princes (an obvious reference to the twelve city-states of Etruria).

The Romans were never particularly well disposed towards the Etruscans, and their traditional resentment may have grown up when Rome was ruled by Etruscan kings. But when they were faced with problems of a religious kind, they accepted unreservedly the in-terpretations of natural phenomena provided by Etruscan priests. In fact they related this tendency to the history of their own origins. Cicero himself wrote:

In the first place, the founder of our city, Romul-us, is said not only to have founded it in obedience to the auspices, but also to have been himself an augur of outstanding skill. After him the other kings also had recourse to soothsayers; and when the kings had been driven out, no state business was ever transacted, whether in time of war or peace, without reference to the auspices.

And as the science of haruspicy seemed to be very successful both in seeking to obtain omens by consulting nature and in understanding and averting evil portents, they introduced the whole of this science from Etruria so that no kind of divination should be neglected (*On Divination*, I, 2).

Especially during the years when the Roman Republic was in gravest danger and portents were the order of the day, it was almost obligatory to consult the Etruscan *haruspices* about them: 'Let them report all prodigies and portents to the Etruscan *haruspices*, if the Senate orders it' (Cicero, *Laws*, 2, IX).

In fact, the body of Roman religion which had grown up during Republican times included the Etruscan science of divination as well as that of the *pontifices* and augurs, with emphasis on averting evil portents. According to the historian Valerius Maximus, writing

Bronze mirror from Tuscania (early third century BC; Museo Archeologico, Florence). Animal entrails are being examined, as the mythical character Tages (identified here as Pava Tarchies) teaches the art of divination to Tarchon (identified here as Tarchunus).

in early Imperial times, the Senate had in the past sent ten young Romans to ten Etruscan cities to learn the principles of divination.

Divination

The Latin phrase *disciplina etrusca* might be translated 'Etruscan science' and was used by the Romans to refer to the whole body of doctrine concerning the interpretation of the divine will as manifested through heavenly signs, certain natural phenomena and portents, and expiatory rites for averting the harmful effects of evil omens.

If natural phenomena were to be interpreted, their physical characteristics had to be observed, but that does not mean that the Etruscans had been led to work out a rational science of natural phenomena. Our chief source of information on the *disciplina etrusca* is Seneca's *Naturales Quaestiones*, in which he takes the Etruscans to task for this mystical attitude of theirs, since it ran counter to the various rational approaches to science which had been adopted ever since the time of Aristotle.

> There is this difference between us Romans and Etruscans. We believe that lightning is caused by clouds colliding, whereas they believe that clouds collide in order to create lightning. Since they attribute everything to the gods, they are led to believe not that events have a meaning because they have happened, but that they happen in order to express a meaning (*Naturales Quaestiones*, II, 32, 2).

In other words, the whole of nature is controlled by the gods, and natural phenomena are simply warnings to men about their future. Every portentous event – that is to say one which did not fall within the normal 'rules' – inevitably had a meaning, which had to be

The man who commissioned the Tomba François at Vulci (see also earlier illustrations) was a member of the fourth-century 'aristocracy' of Vulci, and is shown in the tomb paintings wearing a sumptuously embroidered toga. Here, his slave Arnza *is about to send off a bird. The aristocrat is named as* Vel Saties, *and he gazes upwards as he prepares to draw the appropriate augury from the bird's flight. Divination was in fact a privilege of the cultured class, which also held political power (Villa Albani, Rome).*

discovered if the divine will were to be understood. The *disciplina etrusca* had therefore classified all the 'signs' and their meanings, especially their consequences for the future. This non-rational mentality had brought into being a system of forecasting future events by means of a lore which recorded all past and present 'signs'.

Let us first of all consider Etruscan observations of the heavens, referred to by the Romans as the *templum caeleste*, the dwelling place of the gods. They were divided into four parts by means of two straight lines which crossed at right angles at their mid point and connected the four cardinal points. The north-south line was the *cardo*, and the east-west line the *decumanus*. According to the late Latin poet Martianus Capella, each of the four sectors was itself divided into four parts, each of which was the dwelling of a particular god. There were altogether four celestial gods in the north-east sector, four infernal gods in the north-west sector, and eight terrestrial gods in the eight dwelling places of the south-west and south-east sectors. Because of the way the sun rises and sets, the east was considered a favourable area and the source of life, whereas the west was unfavourable. Hence any portent which appeared in the eastern sector was a good omen, and anything that happened in a westerly direction was an evil omen. And since the most important god, *Tinia*, had his dwelling in the north, any omens from that sector were particularly significant.

According to Servius, who wrote a commentary on Virgil's *Aeneid*, lightning was called *manubia* by the Etruscans, and was sent by the gods from their heavenly dwellings. Only *Tinia*, who in any case occupied three dwellings, could send lightning from dwellings other than his own. According to Seneca, there were altogether nine gods to whom *Tinia* had granted the right to send lightning, while reserving three dwellings for himself for the same purpose. While each of the other gods could only send one kind of lightning, *Tinia* could send three. The first was the *fulmen praesagum* and served as a warning. The second was the *fulmen ostentorium*. It caused fear, but could only be sent after consulting and obtaining the consent of twelve gods (*dii consentes*). In the long digression on the *disciplina etrusca* in which he is paraphrasing Aulus Caecina, Seneca writes: 'This kind of lightning may sometimes have a beneficial effect, but its intention is nevertheless harmful in that it never brings good without also punishing someone.' *Tinia* could only send the third kind of lightning after consulting other gods whom Seneca describes as 'superior and wrapped in mystery' (*superiores et involuti*). This third kind of lightning was the *fulmen peremptorium*, whose effects were always harmful. 'It destroyed'; 'it devastates whatever it strikes and changes the state of public and private affairs'.

The classification of lightning must have been fairly complicated. Lightning was after all 'the most important sign' (*auspicium maximum*), and its effects were considered in relation to the place it struck, the time of its appearance and its consequences for human activities. We have no information about the lightning sent by the other gods, except that five of them are identified by the Latin form of their names as Juno, Minerva, Vulcan, Mars and Saturn.

The *disciplina etrusca* also dealt with rules for carrying out expiatory rites. As in Rome, the place where lightning struck was considered sacred and its tomb was built there, the spot being either fenced in or covered with a small mound of earth. The Romans also used to bury at such spots both objects which had been struck and the bodies of those who had been struck and killed. According to Persius, a first-century AD Latin poet from Volterra, such a spot became 'unlucky' and 'to be

Above: The upper surface of the bronze model of a sheep's liver, found at Settima, near Piacenza. Its inscribed compartments are clearly visible (Museo Civico, Piacenza).

Right: Aule Lecu, *a member of the second-century 'aristocracy' of Volterra, is portrayed on the lid of an urn. He holds a sheep's liver in his left hand, thus showing that he was a priest and* haruspex *(Museo Guarnacci, Volterra).*

avoided' (*triste* and *evitandum*). It provoked fear and could not be walked on. The tomb of the lightning was referred to as *bidental* – a word of obscure origin, which may, however, come from *bidens* meaning a large two-pronged fork, used as a symbol of lightning, or from *bidentes*, an adjective used of adult animals with their second teeth, which were sacrificed when the spot was consecrated.

What Latin literature has to say about the whole system of interpreting nature in the *disciplina etrusca* is contradictory as well as fragmentary. It may be that what information there is refers to different stages in its development and therefore masks the original kernel of doctrine. There is frequent insistence, for example, on the number three and its multiples. *Tinia* has three kinds of lightning, there are nine gods who send lightning, twelve *dii consentes* and probably twelve *dii superiores et involuti*, jointly representing fate, it would seem. And according to Arnobius, they rise and descend together, six male and six female. This cosmology suggests a twelve-sign zodiacal system, and clashes with the division of the heavens into four parts. There is no doubt, however, that the original Etruscan doctrine evolved under the influence of the Greeks, whose scientific study of the universe and of natural phenomena, from Plato onwards, had absorbed a good deal from oriental beliefs. There is evidence for such influence in the 'Piacenza liver', a small second-century bronze model of a sheep's liver; and this leads us into another area of Etruscan divination, namely the examination of animal livers.

According to the Etruscans, the divisions of the heavens have exact equivalents on earth. The macrocosm is reflected in the microcosm, whether the latter is a certain area of land or a very small area such as that of an animal liver.

All the legends about Tages, referred to earlier, together suggest that the examination of animal livers was a specifically Etruscan divinatory technique, as opposed to the interpretation of lightning (*ars fulguratoria*) and portents (*ostenta*) – especially the flight of birds – which are also found in the religion of the Romans and Italic peoples. The way the Etruscan *haruspex* actually examines the liver is different from the Roman method, in that the Etruscan first removes the liver from the animal's body, whereas the Roman method is to examine entrails while they are still attached to the body.

There is an engraving of a *haruspex* inspecting a liver on an early third-century mirror. A young man in *haruspex* costume and wearing a conical cap with a long appendage is holding an animal liver in his hands. An inscription tells us that his name is *Pava Tarchies*. His left foot is resting on a large piece of rock, and his left arm is resting on his left knee. His left hand is holding

logical point of view, because it was thought to be the seat and regulator of the emotions. The convex side of the model liver, corresponding anatomically to the outer surface, is divided into two lobes by a small cord: on the right-hand side is written the word for the sun (*usil*) and on the left-hand side a word which may mean moon (*tivr*). But the most important part is the flat side, with the protruding gall-bladder, *processus piramidalis* and *processus papillaris*. The whole surface is divided into compartments. There are sixteen rectangular ones round the edges, and the inside of the left lobe is divided into six triangular ones from the centre outwards. The right lobe has thirteen compartments which cover the gall-bladder as well. There are five further areas marked out at the centre of the two lobes, giving a total of forty compartments, each of which has the name of a deity engraved on it, often in abbreviated form.

This model liver is some sort of teaching aid. The compartments with names engraved on them must have been for teaching that each part of the liver was supposed to be occupied by a deity, who transferred his dwelling from the heavens to the surface of the liver. Hence the sixteen compartments round the edges of the liver correspond in number to the subdivisions of the heavens.

The ritual for examining entrails was fairly complicated. The chosen animal had to be healthy, and if it followed the priest meekly it was sacrificed. If not, it was rejected. Once the liver had been removed, the first thing to do was to check the dimensions and colour of the whole organ and its parts. The Piacenza liver, however, belongs to a period when Etruscan beliefs were more elaborate, and the work of the *haruspex* more complicated, concerned with the relationship between the division of the heavens and that of terrestrial surfaces. In the case of a liver, for example, the ideal line which divided it into two could correspond to the *cardo* (north-south line) and hence the right lobe was to the east and therefore lucky, whereas the left lobe was to the west and unlucky. Thus the sixteen compartments arranged round the edges of the liver corresponded to the eight dwellings of favourable gods and eight of unfavourable gods. The symbolic significance of the inner compartments has been the subject of much argument, and no firm conclusion has been reached.

The Piacenza liver belongs to a fairly late period when the interpretation of lightning had greatly influenced the examination of livers. An early stage, at which the examination probably meant simply observing the particular physical qualities of the liver, was probably followed later by another when the theological interpretation of astronomical observations caused the divisions of the heavens to be projected on to the liver, with the result that any irregularity in the surface of the liver could provide prognostications for the

the most prominent part of the liver, called the *processus piramidalis*, and the two lobes hang down at the sides like two sacs. Whoever made the engraving has taken care to show up two very important parts of the liver on the left-hand lobe, namely the gall-bladder and the *processus papillaris*, the latter being indicated by means of a small triangle. Other objects show people in the same attitude, for example, there is a late second-century funerary urn on the lid of which is depicted a recumbent nobleman from Volterra with a liver in his hand. He is facing the spectator with the animal entrails to his left.

The best evidence as to the significance of examining livers, however, is provided by the bronze model of a liver found at Piacenza. It is covered in inscriptions in a style of writing which tells us that it comes from Cortona. In ancient lore, the liver was the most important human organ, from a psychological as well as physio-

future, according to the area where an irregularity was found.

The surface of a liver fits perfectly well into the three categories of area for observation as defined quite clearly by Varro: the heavens, the earth and the underworld. So not only the surface of a liver, but any consecrated area, whether bounded by posts or trees (there are also known cases of stone *cippi*), or surrounded by wooden walls or tapes, could be considered an appropriate terrestrial space. A *templum* was thus a defined space for prayer and for receiving omens, where the priest or whoever waited for heavenly 'signs' had his place. As in the case of lightning, the observer had to be at the ideal spot, that is to say on the north-south line and with his back to the southern hemisphere, so that the favourable area was to his right and the unfavourable to his left. As a consecrated terrestrial space, the *templum* was also conceived as a vital point of reference for ceremonial purposes in relation to the city. Even though it might not occupy an exactly central position in the city, it was the ideal and religious centre of the whole *pomerium*, that is to say the space along the city walls which was also considered sacred. The heavens were the priest's mental point of reference, and the plan of the *templum* on the ground reflected the organization of the heavens in a formal way. Thus the gods also had their specific dwellings on earth. This may well be another case in which 'signs' were observed first for their individual characteristics (what kinds of birds were seen, what their cries were like, and so on), and only at a later stage for the place or direction from which they came. Among the few relics of Etruscan words which have come down to us through ancient writers, there is a fairly substantial group of names of birds. They probably belong to the Etruscan tradition of augury, for the augurs were priests who interpreted the flight of birds,

Right: Bronze lituus *(36cm. long) from a tomb at Cerveteri (early sixth century* BC; *Museo di Villa Giulia, Rome). At this period the* lituus *had a dual political and religious significance, because these two functions had not yet become separated.*

Left: Sanctuary at Pieve a Socana (Arezzo). The church is an eleventh-century Romanesque building. Underneath it have been discovered the remains of the foundations of an Etruscan temple whose entrance lies beneath the apse of the church. In front of the temple is a rectangular altar (5 × 3.75m.) made of blocks of stone cut to shape and held together by means of metal clamps (fifth century BC*).*

and augury must have flourished in Etruria as it did in Rome and elsewhere among the Italic peoples.

These relics of Etruscan vocabulary also include the names of animals and plants, and indeed one branch of the interpretation of natural phenomena included the observation and explanation of anything out of the ordinary in the animal or vegetable kingdoms. Even trees were involved in the basic opposition between good and evil which operated throughout the universe. Thus one kind of plant, if it had white sap and was edible, was lucky while another, if wild and with dark sap, was unlucky. Anything abnormal could provide information about the future, either for an individual or in a more general sense; and it was the task of priests not only to interpret this abnormality but to show how such a portent might be expiated; and their answers might even be in verse.

When Livy writes about the many portents which occurred during the course of Roman history, he gives the impression that it was fairly normal to consult Etruscan priests about their significance and the necessary expiatory rites. An explanation was sought for loud bangs, musical sounds, monsters, or anything else of an unusual kind, and the attitude of the Etruscan *haruspices* to such phenomena was usually of an out-and-out reactionary kind. In other words, they unequivocally supported the kind of established authority which, in Rome, consisted of the senatorial aristocracy.

In the first century BC, the whole science of divination was referred to as *haruspicina* in Rome, although the term must originally have been limited to the interpretation of animal entrails, as one can see from a funerary inscription discovered at Pesaro, in which the dead man is described in Latin as *haruspex* and *fulguriator* (the corresponding Etruscan terms are *netśvis* and *trutnvt*), indicating that he was an interpreter of entrails and lightning. As early as the fourth century, the *haruspices* belonged to a priestly college, which may have come into being under the influence of the Roman Senate; and in the first century BC they carried out a variety of different divinatory activities. This system guaranteed continuity in a branch of learning for which one was selected and trained from early childhood. The appropriate training was carried out in individual Etruscan cities, and it was the sons of aristocratic families who were educated to take their place in the official priestly organization which the Romans called the 'ordo of the sixty *haruspices*'. Positions in this body were handed down from father to son, and the conservative, pro-Roman attitude which was typical of it is definitely connected with the social position of its members in their home towns. Hence it was very unlikely, from the third century onwards, that the Etruscan ruling class would adopt any kind of revolutionary attitude in their dealings with Rome.

The role of the priestly class within the city-state became more clearly defined in the sixth century, and must have been directly related to the aristocratic background of its members. According to Censorius, a Roman scholar of the third century AD, the inspection of livers was a science which came directly from the ancient kings known as *lucumones*; and according to Livy all the priests responsible for looking after temples were aristocrats. Under the Empire, the Etruscan *haruspices* had become romanized and belonged to the class of knights.

The badge of office of the priest was a kind of staff with a curved end, called a *lituus*, and examples dating to the first half of the sixth century have been found. According to Roman annalists, it was in use as early as the time of the kings of Rome. Thus the augur who accompanied Numa Pompilius to the citadel in order to seek omens on his appointment as king of Rome carried in his right hand a 'small curved staff, without knots'. From the late sixth century onwards, figures carrying a *lituus* are commonly found in Etruria, both on small votive bronzes and funerary *stelae*. But in the earliest architectural terracottas from the 'palace' at Murlo, the *lituus* is still an attribute of the 'chief', who represents both political and religious authority.

The priestly class, then, develops at the same time as the city itself, when public cults were coming to be recognized and the power of kings was beginning to break down. As time went on, it became possible to specialize within the priestly class. There is a series of third-century coins bearing on the obverse the head of a *haruspex* with his conical cap, and on the reverse his sacrificial instruments; the axe and the knife. Whereas the *haruspex* was called *netśvis*, the priests responsible for public cults were called *cepen*, and it is quite likely that there were differences of rank among them, for in some late inscriptions we find a reference to *spurana cepen* (public priest) as opposed to the more generic term *cepen*.

It is reasonable to suppose that priests were also responsible for preserving other forms of learning, as in Rome. The calculation of time, for example, was something which had its place within the total deterministic vision of the cosmos. Censorinus tells us that the Etruscan ritual books contained a specific doctrine relating to the *saecula*, that is to say the period of time allotted to states – including Etruria – as well as to individuals. According to the ritual books, the maximum period allotted to Etruria was ten *saecula*, which had begun towards the end of the second millennium BC. A *saeculum* did not consist of a fixed number of years, but its end was heralded by prodigies such as comets or mysterious trumpet blasts. The prophecy of Vegoia (see page 46) speaks of the end of the eighth

Early fifth-century figures carrying a lituus *probably represent priests. They no longer carry weapons – the symbols of political power.*
Right: Relief on a gravestone found in the territory of Florence (early fifth century; Museo Archeologico, Florence).
Left: Bronze Etruscan statuette from Isola di Fano, near Fossombrone (end of the sixth century BC; Museo Archeologico, Florence).

'century'. If, as seems likely, this can be dated to the beginning of the first century BC, then it looks as though the Etruscan priests were not far out in calculating when Etruria would come to an end.

The passage of time was in any case recorded in calendars, which used a system of computation based on the lunar cycle. In fact, Roman scholars who were puzzled about the etymology of the word 'Ides', meaning the middle of the month, claimed that it was of Etruscan origin and was called *itus* in that language. The subdivision of the year into twelve months was certainly known to the Etruscans, whose calendar may have influenced that of the Romans at the time of the kings; and we know the names of eight months. One of them appears in the early fifth-century Pyrgi inscriptions.

Sanctuaries and Public Cults

The names of the gods engraved on the sixteen outer compartments of the Piacenza liver ought to provide us with some information about the Etruscan pantheon in the second century. Among the great heavenly gods we find the names *Tin(ia), Ani* and *Uni* (Jupiter, Janus and Juno), while the gods of nature include *Selva(ns), Fufluns* and *Neth(uns)* (Sylvanus, Bacchus and Neptune), and those of the underworld include *Tivus* and *Vetis* (Luna and Vejovis); but some of the other names are difficult to identify.

It is usual to distinguish the Etruscan gods by their names, and to identify the Roman gods to which they correspond by means of the very frequent images which appear on vases and mirrors from the fourth century onwards. One group of gods is thought to be of specifically Etruscan origin. *Tinia, Turan, Fufluns, Turms, Sethlans, Thesan, Cautha* and *Tiv* correspond to

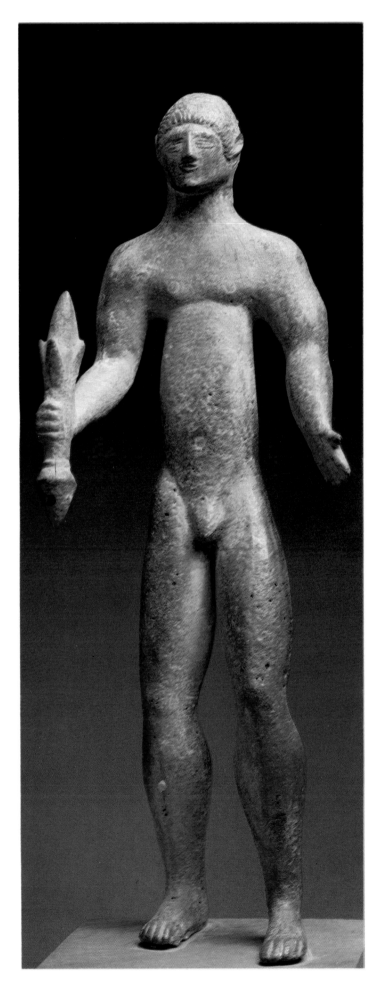

Images of the gods in human form were brought to Etruria by the Greeks, and the Etruscan pantheon tends to adopt Greek models in its iconography. Thus the Greek image of Zeus comes to correspond to that of the Etruscan celestial god Tinia, *who is usually represented grasping a thunderbolt.*
Right: Small bronze figure of Tinia *with a thunderbolt. From Firenzuola in the Tusco-Emilian Apennines (fifth century* BC*; Museo dell' Accademia Etrusca, Cortona).*
Left: Terracotta head of Tinia, *from Falerii (late fifth century* BC*; Museo di Villa Giulia, Rome). This head is modelled on the Zeus of Phidias.*

the Roman Jupiter, Venus, Bacchus, Mars, Vulcan, Aurora, Daughter of the Sun, and Luna. *Voltumna* may correspond to the Roman Vertumnus, and was particularly honoured at Volsinii (Orvieto). It may well be that *Voltumna* became a 'national' deity at a fairly late stage, probably in historical times, when the political 'league' of Etruscan cities came into being (see page 18). Another group of gods has clear affinities with Italic religion, and is evidence of the long-established relationship between the Etruscans and the other peoples of central Italy. The gods in question are: *Menerva, Uni* (related to *Iuno* or Juno), *Maris* (Mars), *Nethuns, Selvans* (Sylvanus) and *Ani* (Janus). And one last group has names of Greek origin and is to be related to the historically identified period when Greek cults came to Italy: *Aritimi* (Artemis), *Apulu* (Apollo) and *Hercle* (Heracles) are the most important of these. *Aita* (Hades) and *Pheripnai* (Persephone) came later.

Some of these gods are of very ancient origin. *Tinia*, for example, has the typical characteristics of an all-seeing, heavenly deity, partly because of his position in the heavens; and his power to send warnings and punishment is expressed in the form of natural phenomena such as lightning. It is more difficult, on the other hand, to pinpoint the characteristics of *Voltumna*, who seems to have had connections with agriculture. A comparison with the Roman god Vertumnus, who also appears to have been connected with agriculture, could be used to support the theory that *Voltumna* was a sort of *Tinia* with agricultural attributes, especially if one compares his name with that of the mythical *Volta*, whom Porsenna conjured out of the earth, according to a legend reported by classical writers.

These gods belong to cults which may well go back deep into prehistory, but in historical times, as we have seen, the Etruscan pantheon seems to be particularly rich and varied. Hence one finds not only phrases referring to groups of gods such as the *dii consentes* and the *dii superiores et involuti*, which also occur in the interpretation of lightning, but also phrases referring to specific *aisar* (deities) in a collective role, such as those in the Zagreb ritual book.

How gods came to be grouped into threes is a matter for debate. It is sometimes held that this phenomenon is of Etruscan origin or came to the Etruscans under Italic influence. The little evidence we have suggests that it is better not to make generalizations about the way the gods were grouped, especially since there is reliable evidence for the cult of triads only for Rome, and this evidence is not confined to the time of the Etruscan kings. It may well be that the cities of Etruria, like those of Greece, developed their theology independently. In Etruscan Rome, we find such groups of three deities in the Capitoline cult of Jupiter, Juno and Minerva; whereas in early Republican times there was the 'ple-

Above: Marble head, possibly of a male deity. Larger than life size (circa 480 BC; Collezione Lorenzini, Volterra).

Right: Marble statue of the deity Vei, *from the Cannicella sanctuary outside Orvieto. The statue was originally an East Greek* kouros, *and was adapted and given female attributes in Etruria for religious purposes (late sixth century BC; Museo Faina, Orvieto).*

beian' cult of Ceres, Liberus and Libera. However, such groups are not random ones – they require an explanation in historical and theological terms. Similarly, the classification of the Etruscan gods provided by the fifth-century AD Latin poet Martianus Capella belongs to a tradition which is too late and has been subject to too many accretions to be completely reliable.

Those cults which we know of through literary sources or from archaeological evidence seem rather to be related to the specifically Greek idea of deities who protect the city-state. A significant example is that of the temple on the citadel at Veii, where the citizens worshipped *Uni*, the goddess who was taken to Rome in 396 BC after the destruction of Veii, and there worshipped as *Iuno Regina* (Queen Juno). Other cults at Veii, such as that of *Menerva* or an underworld goddess whom Roman settlers later identified as Ceres, were carried on outside the city walls.

We lack evidence of this kind for Cerveteri, although there must have been a temple dedicated to *Uni* in the southern part of the city (a temple still frequented by Greeks at the beginning of the third century), as well as cults of oracles carried on outside the urban area. The two temples at Pyrgi were built with an interval of fifty years between them (the first dates to the end of the sixth century and the second to about 460 BC), and probably represent two different stages in the history of the city. The first may have been built by the 'tyrant' *Thefarie Velianas* and as such represents the fulfilment of a vow made to *Uni-Astarte*, his personal protectress. The other may be specifically for the city itself, and with its three cells may be evidence of a series of cults to various gods, including *Tinia* and Aurora (*Thesan*).

At Tarquinia, the most important cult was practised in the *Ara della Regina* temple, which was probably dedicated to *Uni*, since, in Roman times, it was turned into a temple to *Iuno Regina*. There is also evidence of a cult of Tarchon, the legendary founder of the city.

The principal cults at Volsinii (Orvieto) seem to have been those of underworld deities who were related to the earth and fertility. The temple inside the city can still be seen in the district called Belvedere, and was dedicated to *Tinia* in an infernal rather than a celestial role. Outside the city, in the locality now called Cannicella, there was a sanctuary dedicated to *Vei* – an unidentified deity whose characteristics seem to have been strictly Aphrodisian. The sanctuary of *Voltumna*, on the other hand, has not yet been found.

In places which were much frequented by merchants, especially on the coast, cults must have developed thick and fast. By the first century BC, Populonia had been more or less abandoned by its population, but, according to Strabo, a number of sanctuaries and shrines were still standing. There were a number of cults at Gravisca, the port of Tarquinia: in the sixth century the Greeks worshipped Hera, Aphrodite and Apollo, and the Etruscans later continued the cult of Aphrodite, identifying her with their own goddess *Turan*. Similarly, the cult of *Uni* at the end of the sixth century at Pyrgi was extended to include the Phoenician *Astarte*, evidently because there were Carthaginians about the town, and dedicatory inscriptions suggest a great number of different cults. It is almost certain that sacred prostitution was carried on at the sanctuary.

In other words, every city must have had its principal, official cult, and the principal temple within the city was its essential point of reference. Varro tells us that the Romans began giving their gods a specific physical image only 170 years after the foundation of Rome (about 580 BC, therefore), and the same may be true of the Etruscans, for it was substantial contact with the Greek world and its figurative art which caused them to give their gods the characteristics of men. At an early

stage, cult statues must have been made of perishable materials. Pliny the Elder recalls that there was a very ancient statue of Jupiter at Populonia made out of the wood of a vine. The cult statue of Jupiter Capitolinus, which Vulca made during the reign of Tarquinius Priscus, was of terracotta, and from time to time was repainted with red lead. At Orvieto at the end of the sixth century, the statue of a Greek *kouros* (young man) was taken into service in a new role as the goddess *Vea*. The earliest images of gods used as votive gifts belong to the end of the sixth century.

The creation of public cults inside cities brought with it a series of regulations concerning the sacred areas. This is confirmed by a passage from the *libri rituales*. Even before this, it appears that the founding of a city had to be carried out according to strict rules. Thus Roman annals attribute the ritual used by Romulus in founding Rome to the Etruscans. Full details of the ritual were explained to him. A circular trench was dug and into it were thrown the first fruits of all those foods considered useful and necessary for human survival. This spot was called a *mundus* and became the central point of the city. The line of the city walls, namely the *pomerium*, inside which was to be the urban area, was traced by a plough drawn by a bull and a cow. This line was sacred and might not be crossed, and so, as the plough dug its furrow, it was raised at the points where the city gates were to be. The internal subdivision of the urban area was also carried out in accordance with precise rules, using a *groma* (an instrument for land surveying) and applying the principles of *inauguratio*. In this sense it is significant that, at both Marzabotto and Spina, *cippi* for surveying purposes are buried under the roadway at crossroads.

We have reliable evidence about the founding and placing of temples from the first-century BC Roman architect Vitruvius, who has this to say near the beginning of his work, *Architecture* (I, 7):

> Having laid out the streets and squares, we have next to deal with the choice of sites for public buildings, that is to say for temples, the forum and all other public places. If the walls are close to the sea, the site for the forum should be chosen near the harbour, but if the city is inland, the forum should be placed in the middle of the town. As for the temples, those dedicated to deities who protect the city, and those dedicated to Jupiter, Juno and Minerva, should be on the very highest point, commanding a view of the greater part of the city walls. The temple of Mercury should be near the forum, or, like those of Isis and Serapis, in the market; those of Apollo and Bacchus should be near the theatre; that of Hercules at the circus, if there is no gymnasium or amphitheatre; that of Mars should be outside

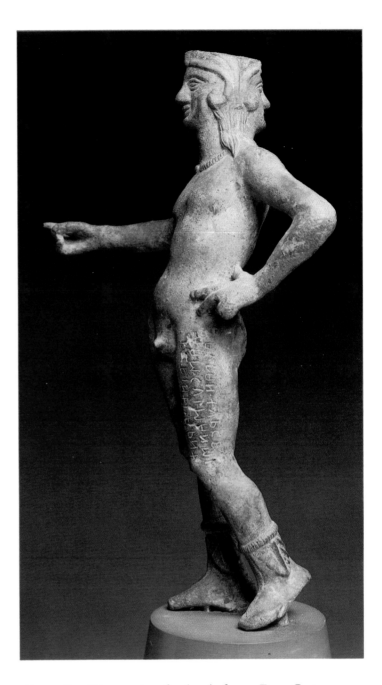

Above: Small bronze two-faced male figure. From Cortona (third to second century BC; Museo dell' Accademia Etrusca, Cortona). One of a pair of figures offered to the deities Selvans (Sylvanus) and Culsans.

Left: Small bronze votive figure of a warrior (first half of the fifth century BC; Museo Archeologico, Florence). This figure is probably intended to represent the god of war Maris (Mars).

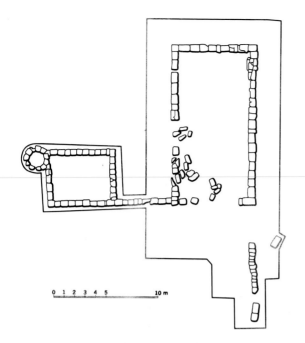

the city, but near the military training ground; that of Venus should be outside the city, near the harbour. The writings of the Etruscan *haruspices* also say that the sanctuaries of Venus, Vulcan and Mars should be situated outside the city, so that young men and married women may not become accustomed to the pleasures of the flesh, and so that city buildings shall be free from the danger of fire when the power of Vulcan is called forth with religious sacrifices. If the temple of Mars is placed outside the city, that will prevent the citizens from taking up arms against one another and will also protect the walls against enemies and the dangers of war. The sanctuary of Ceres should also be placed outside the city, so that no one shall enter it except for the purpose of sacrifice; for it is a place that should be respected in accordance with the appropriate principles of morals and ethics. As for the other gods, sites for their temples should be chosen in accordance with the nature of the sacrifices to be offered to them.

This passage clearly involves a whole variety of rules, since it not only refers to exotic, Alexandrian gods such as Isis and Serapis, but also buildings of Greek origin, such as the gymnasium and theatre, which Vitruvius associates with gods of Greek origin such as Apollo, Bacchus and Hercules. The second part of the passage, however, is inspired by the precepts of the *disciplina etrusca*. The choice of position for the most important temples seems, moreover, to be confirmed by the earliest archaeological evidence, such as that found at Veii, Volterra and Marzabotto.

The same set of rules must also have laid down the orientation of temples and the sacrificial altars in front of them. The altars had to face east, and had to be situ-

ated at forty-five degrees to the temple façade; and indeed the majority of Etruscan temples do seem to be oriented towards the south-east.

At the end of the first century BC, the temple with three *cellae* was considered typical of Etruscan sacred buildings. Vitruvius tells us the principles on which such a temple was built (IV, 7). The ratio between long and short sides had to be 6:5; and the temple was divided lengthwise into two parts. The front part was reserved for the *vestibulum* and the rear part for the *cellae*. These were arranged with relative widths 3:4:3, and the columns of the façade of the *vestibulum* had to be aligned with the walls. The wood and terracotta elevation and roof of the temple also had to obey a strict series of mathematical rules. Vitruvius found the results aesthetically unsatisfactory. 'The temples make an impression which reminds me of a man with a large, low and broad head, standing with his legs wide apart.' Certainly the columns were far apart, and the roof structure was heavy, with its many terracotta or gilded bronze statues. The impression was possibly similar to that of the temple of Jupiter Capitolinus in Rome, or the Portonaccio temple at Veii, from which there have been preserved many terracotta statues which must have been used to decorate the top of the roof, arranged in groups to represent episodes in the saga of Apollo.

Temple altars were placed in front of the façade. Since this was the most important kind of altar, it was often of monumental proportions (such as those at Veii or Fiesole, or in the recently discovered sanctuary at Socana in the province of Arezzo), and was conceived differently, from an architectural point of view, from Greek altars, although it preserved their orientation and, in part, their plan. The Greek altar had a vertical profile, whereas the Etrusco-Italic type had large matched mouldings on the base and cornice. This was the sacrificial altar; beside it was sometimes placed an altar for libations (for example, at Veii and Pyrgi). The latter was cylindrical in shape and had an inner channel which led to the ground. In this way drinks or other liquids went straight down and wet the ground, thereby pleasing some underworld deity. Many altars of this kind, with an inscription which specifically names the god concerned, are found in the vicinity of Volsinii, where even *Tinia* had lost his celestial characteristics and taken on those typical of an infernal god.

Not all cults, however, can have been carried on at monumental buildings. Official ceremonies related to urban cults must have been preceded by a stage when ceremonies were dominated by the upper classes. What sacred places of this kind looked like can perhaps be partly guessed by looking at the remains of a few small 'rural' sanctuaries. There is one at Monte Acuto Ragazza in the Apennines, towards Bologna, and its *templum* simply consisted of a roofless rectangular structure

only 4 metres (13 feet) square, enclosing the sacred area and its altar. This fifth-century temple is a very important piece of evidence, because it bears witness to a stage in the development of religious life when the influence of the Greek world had not yet brought to Etruria a monumental conception of the palace of worship, seen as a direct reflection of urban organization.

It is sanctuaries of this type which give us the best chance of assessing votive offerings. Especially in northern Etruria, one continually finds offerings of small bronzes which are a direct representation of the donor, including those attributes which define his social role. In pre-urban times, figures of warriors predominate; then come figures of athletes, which constitute a strictly Greek and direct expression of the psychological and physical qualities of the aristocracy; and then, in the late fifth century, come images of gods such as *Tinia* or *Hercle*. Inscriptions on these images

One of the most interesting city sanctuaries is the Ara della Regina temple inside the urban area of Tarquinia. As in the case of other similar temples, this one has been rebuilt more than once, but its earliest form seems to go back to the first half of the sixth century BC. What is now visible is the fourth-century BC version, to which further additions were made and altars added up to and into Roman times. Compared with the simple plan of the Archaic temple at Veii (see plan on preceding page), which was also intramural, the temple at Tarquinia was a more complex structure, with a podium and a single cella with a colonnaded vestibule.

are rare. There is, however, a late sixth-century small bronze figure of a warrior, found at Ravenna, which bears the words 'Thucer Hermenas dedicated (me)', and a second-century bronze image of a deity with two faces, found at Cortona, on which is written 'Vel Quintio (son) of Arntni dedicated this offering to Culsans.'

The offering might take a more modest form, particularly in early times. In the Portonaccio sanctuary at Veii, the commonest offerings, even in the first half of the sixth century, seem to be pottery. There is quite a collection of bucchero and painted vases with dedicatory inscriptions, in which the formula *mini muluvanice* ('gave me') is very common; and it is perhaps more than a coincidence that the leaders of urban communities were involved in these cults. Even Aulus Vibenna, whom we have had occasion to meet before (page 85), offered the local deity a bucchero chalice.

Even less costly were the terracotta offerings which seem to have been widely used in southern Etruria. One not very substantial group consists of small human figures with specific attributes such as weapons or a lyre. Or they may be represented seated as 'mothers' with a baby in their arms. Such figures may have been ambivalent in function in the sense that they could represent human beings or their divine counterparts, such as Mars, Apollo or the mother goddess. A very substantial group of offerings, on the other hand, consists of representations of parts of the human body (heads, arms, legs, feet and intestines). These seem to have their origin in a popular form of religious feeling which was widespread in the whole of central Italy from the fourth century onwards. Almost all the gods, regardless of their healing qualities, seem to have been involved in offerings of this kind, which occur in urban as well as rural cults.

Two small bronze female figures making offerings. The one on the left dates to the Orientalizing period, and the one below to the Hellenistic age. They were dedicated to a deity in a sacred place and then buried as the property of the deity concerned. Although there are about four centuries between these two figures, the iconography remains unchanged (Museo Archeologico, Florence).

Left: Fragment of a model temple from Orvieto (fifth century BC; Museo Archeologico, Florence). The decoration of an actual building is represented quite realistically, with tiles, antefixes and a cornice over the pediment.

Once the number of offerings had become so large as to fill available space and cause obstacles in buildings, they were deposited in specially dug pits, which are often found near major sanctuaries. Most of the information we have about the nature of the ceremonies carried out in temples comes from the longest Etruscan texts we possess, namely the tile from S. Maria Capua Vetere (see page 81) and the linen book used for wrapping the mummy now in the Zagreb museum.

The text from S. Maria Capua Vetere is shorter than the other, but older (it dates from the fifth century BC), and contains a series of formulae which begin with the name of a deity and specify different types of offering to be made by priests, and perhaps also by families. The text of the Zagreb book (dating to the first century BC), however, is organized differently. In the best preserved part, the formulae begin with a date and go on to describe the religious ceremonies to be carried out at that time. The 'literary' nature of the text has been mentioned earlier. Judging by some of the interpretations proposed, the liturgical aspect of the ritual is based on specified offerings being made to the gods. The formulae are fixed and all begin with the statement that on a certain day in a certain month, offerings to a specified deity must be made and consecrated. The principal gods in this particular liturgy are the *eiser sic seuc*, or *sic seuc* gods, *Crapsti* (Grabovius) and *Nethuns* (Neptune). Offerings are made to protect the city (*spur*) and the nation (*methlum*) and consist basically of libations of wine (*vinum*) and the first fruits of corn, which were sometimes presented on litters (*cletram*). There were certainly also offerings involving the slaughter of animals. The earliest images showing episodes connected with the life of settlements controlled by the aristocracy are found in the second half of the seventh century, and they include, for example, offerings of pigs and rams at propitiatory ceremonies before battle.

Among the commonest types of votive offering from the end of the fourth century up to the period of Romanization are terracotta representations of heads, limbs and other parts of the body, mass-produced by means of stamps and moulds. They were dedicated to those gods who were thought to be concerned with human health. These two examples – the head of a man and a uterus – may have come from a sanctuary at Veii. They are now in the Museo Archeologico in Florence.

The Etruscan View of Life after Death

Religion had its private aspect as well, and in this sense could be related to the individual or the family. Perhaps for the Etruscans, as for the Romans, each person had his own 'genius' who accompanied him throughout his life – the life span being divided into groups of seven years each. The seventh year acted as a kind of step which separated one period of life from the next, and brought with it dangers of every kind. After reaching the age of seventy, it was no longer possible to have 'signs' from the gods, for the span of human life had then reached its end.

Family cults were particularly associated with the *Lares*, that is to say the shades of the family's ancestors, and more will be said about that later on; but there must also have been cults of 'minor' deities which were well

adapted to the traditional aristocratic structure of society. Thus a goddess *Uni Ursmnei* and another called *Iuno*, of the *Ursmna* family, were worshipped at Chiusi, and deities with two-part names were common in the region of Perugia, the second part of the name being clearly of aristocratic type. *Lasa Achunuma, Lasa Vecuvia* and *Cautha Achuia* are examples. The cult of one's ancestors was clearly the most ancient kind of worship, and there is very interesting evidence of this in the tomb interiors of the cemetery at Cerveteri. Inside one plain mid-seventh-century tomb is the sculpted figure of a seated, bearded man, and in another tomb, more complex in plan, a whole chamber is devoted to this cult. Cut out of rock are five rectangular seats on which there must have been placed five terracotta statues, in front of whom were two tables. These figures were an idealized representation of the family ancestors, rendered in the style characteristic of the Orientalizing period. Two chairs with curved backs were arranged in another wall and in the opposite wall was a small altar, parallele-piped in shape, with three cavities in its upper surface. This type was for multiple private offerings, and occurs again at a later period.

The cult of one's ancestors forms part of the Etruscans' most ancient traditions, and is clearly related to the idea of the founder of the family, which is typical of aristocratic society. Even in late Etruscan times, when the tombs at Tarquinia are of considerable dimensions, dedicatory inscriptions refer to the forefathers of the dead, and there are some cases of altars inside a tomb, such as, for example, the second-century Tomb of the Typhon.

The imposing seventh- and sixth-century tombs at Cerveteri sometimes have a ramp or flight of steps on one side, which must have led from ground level to the top of the funerary tumulus, where ceremonies in honour of the dead were performed. Even in the most

Left: Bronze votive image (third to second century BC *; Museo di Villa Giulia, Rome). In this case the figure making the offering is identified as a* haruspex, *whose cloak is held by a* fibula *placed at the centre. (*Haruspices *were not allowed to use knots or strings.) He also wears the characteristic pointed cap of the* haruspex.

Right: Interior of the Tomba delle Cinque Sedie at Cerveteri. The tomb contains a number of different rooms, the one shown here being perhaps intended for the cult of ancestors. There are five seats cut out of the rock, on which five terracotta figures were intended to sit (second half of the seventh century BC*).*

ancient cube-tombs in the area of the rock cemeteries, there were steps at the sides to give access to the platform below on which ceremonies were held.

Although this is an area in which wide differences of cultural level can be detected, there is no doubt that the cult of the dead played an important part in the Etruscan mentality. During the Iron Age, the dead person was viewed very much as an individual, and the Villanovan biconical urn, sometimes covered with a helmet instead of the traditional cover-bowl, is an early schematic representation of his physical form. The spread of inhumation in southern Etruria in the seventh century coincides with the use of chamber tombs which are a deliberate representation of a dwelling. In the inland part of Etruria – and especially at Chiusi – where cremation persists, there is evidence of a tradition which comes directly from the Iron Age. The urn has anthropomorphic decoration and becomes a symbol of the dead person, who is always buried with the furnishings and insignia of his rank. It is here in particular that figurative evidence confirms that death is seen as a sad occurrence: a painful separation. Burials are often accompanied by vases decorated with a whole series of small weeping figures, in the round, encircling a central figure which presumably represents the dead man, and whose importance in relation to the others is conveyed by his larger dimensions. Funerary containers in human shape, known as canopic urns, are provided with a seat and often have individual furnishings such as small bronze tables on which food and drink may have been placed in order to provide the dead person with whatever was necessary for his survival in life. In many cities, the shape of the tomb was a symbolic representation of the dead person's home, aiming to recreate his home surroundings, and offerings of food which have been found are also part of the funerary rites.

During the second half of the sixth century, the banquet theme gradually increases in frequency in painted tombs at Tarquinia, and in the fifth century it becomes standard. Since painted tombs constitute barely two per cent of all tombs, it is clear that they are directly representative of the urban aristocracy. An open-air banquet is shown, with those present reclining on couches as they listen to musicians or watch dancers, jugglers or competitive games. Other funerary monuments of this same period provide a more realistic representation of the cult of the dead and the various parts of the funeral ceremony. The dead person is shown being laid on a bed in the presence of weeping mourners, being transported on a cart with a procession of relatives, and then there are the games and dances and the banquet, which is perhaps the final part of the ceremony. Series of scenes of this kind, describing the various parts of a single ceremony, can be found in the form of reliefs on funerary *cippi* from Chiusi, mostly dating to the late sixth and early fifth century. By this time the funerary ceremonies of the aristocracy combine ancient traditions, such as the mourners, with more recent elements such as the procession, games and banquet, which appear contemporaneously in aristocratic tombs in states on the outer edges of the Greek world, such as Lycia.

The first part of the ceremony is concerned with specific rites related to the dead person, whereas the second part, although it involves commemorating the dead person, seems to be primarily concerned with the living. As they watch sporting competitions or partake of a communal meal, they collectively regain confidence, from a psychological point of view, in their own physical existence, thereby exorcising the idea of death. The representation of these rituals in visual form, however, gives them a symbolic significance in which

Above: Gravestone from Chiusi (500–480 BC; Museo Barracco, Rome). A dead woman is shown being laid out on a bed. Of the three women standing round her, one is in the act of mourning, while a second is bringing ointments. Standing at the foot of the bed is a man playing the double pipes.

Left: Inscribed handle of a ritual shovel. From San Feliciano (Perugia). Now in the Museo Archeologico, Florence. The inscription dates to the third or second century BC, and reads as follows: 'This is the shovel [for the rites] of Kavtha Achuia. Aulus Numna dedicated it.' The deity referred to in the text is an infernal one, but the addition of the family name Achu indicates that the cult concerned was aristocratic.

each element of the ritual has its figurative counterpart; and the choice of the banquet as the dominant theme in fifth-century tombs at Tarquinia is probably a reflection of the ostentatious part that banquets played in real life.

An examination of the decorative images and furnishings in tombs makes it clear that in the fourth century – and perhaps a little earlier in inland cities – ideas about death were changing. In tomb paintings at Orvieto, the banquet is transferred to the other world and the occupant of the tomb arrives there in his cart with all the insignia of his rank. He is admitted to a sort of permanent banquet which is also attended by his ancestors under the watchful eye of Hades and Persephone, the principal deities of the underworld. In the Tomba dell'Orco II at Tarquinia, the dead are actually placed in heroic surroundings. Along the walls are to be seen not only

The Tomba del Tifone at Tarquinia (mid-second century BC). The interior has a strikingly monumental appearance and could contain the bodies of an entire family group. In front of the pilaster is an altar for funerary sacrifices, and at the top is a long inscribed dedication which indicates, among other things, that the tomb belonged to the Pumpu *family.*

the two infernal deities, but also the great heroes of the Greek myths – Agamemnon, Theseus and so on – who are now condemned to idleness. In other words, these images are pervaded by a pessimistic view of the other world, probably under the influence of that of Greek culture. Funerary scenes are now peopled with infernal deities such as *Charun* (Charon: a livid demon with human features but with a hooked nose and an animal-like face), or *Vanth* (a coldly beautiful winged female figure). *Charun* holds a hammer as a sign of the pain he inflicts on the dead, and *Vanth* has a scroll as a symbol of the prescribed destiny of every mortal. But there are other demons in the nether world, such as *Tuchulcha*, wrapped in snakes and with a monstrous face, and *Culsu* with her torch, one of the many winged furies. These figures sometimes appear in non-funerary scenes (for example in Hellenistic temple pediments), where they appear to be symbolic figures warning men of the evil destiny which even the heroes of Greek myths finally meet.

The scene of the transportation of the dead body now becomes a symbolic representation of the dead person's journey to the other world. The journey begins after the dead person's family have been left behind, and he travels in a chariot, on horseback or on foot. It ends in a world where the dead may be subjected to torture. Such themes seem to predominate on most third- and second-century sarcophagi and funerary urns. Under Greek influence, the Etruscan view of life after death becomes clearly defined, and it is in this situation that one finds evidence for new beliefs and rituals concerning the destiny of man after death. According to Arnobius, a Christian writer of the fourth century AD, the Etruscan Books of the Dead showed that they believed that when the blood of certain animals had been offered to certain underworld deities, the dead became divine as *dii animales*, so called because they emanated directly from the dead. These *dii animales* became the household gods, corresponding to the Roman *Lares* and *Penates*. In other words, one's ancestors became deities who protected the household. In second-century dwellings at Vetulonia, there have indeed been found domestic images of *Lares* on small stone bases, wearing cloaks and with heads surrounded by rays.

This new mentality seems to have taken root in the fourth century, and accounts very well for the spread of Dionysiac cults in Etruria, especially among the aristocracy. Those who took part in the secret ceremonies in honour of Dionysus, during which they became, as it were, ritually possessed, were guaranteed as initiates a kind of escape from reality through wine intoxication, and this could foreshadow a happy fate in the world beyond. Hence Dionysiac themes become

Top right: Alabaster urn from Volterra (early second century BC; *Museo Guarnacci, Volterra). In the centre is a man about to leave for the other world. This is rendered symbolically by the arrival of a man on horseback leading a riderless horse. The dead man will mount this horse and travel in the company of his dead mother and father, the latter also on horseback. The identity of the parents is established by the inscription.*

Right: Red-figure krater *from Carmignano (Florence) for holding ashes (circa 330* BC; *Museo Archeologico, Florence). The followers of Bacchus believed in life after death, and Bacchic cults became particularly deep-rooted in Etruria during the fourth and third centuries* BC. *Hence the figures in a Dionysiac procession on this vase made at Volterra.*

119

very frequent in fourth-century vase painting. Vases designed strictly for funerary purposes abound in Bacchic processions, and on some sarcophagi the dead are represented as followers of Dionysus, with *thyrsi* (Bacchic wands) in their hands. In 186 BC, when the Roman Senate issued a decree abolishing bacchanals because they were considered a danger to the state, the followers of Bacchus in Etruria were also organized in associations whose structure was such that they might also be considered a danger to the state. Nevertheless, there are earlier inscriptions concerning many members of the aristocracy which record their position in these associations along with their municipal offices. 'He was a praetor of Etruria and a priest; he was a praetor once, and he was a priest of the cult of Bacchus', declares an epitaph on a sarcophagus at Tarquinia. And on another, an inscription states, 'Larth Statlane son of Vel died at the age of 36. He was a priest of the followers of Bacchus.'

Top right: Tufa urn from Volterra (early first century BC; Museo Guarnacci, Volterra). A dead man wearing a cloak appears to a woman (his wife) lying on a bed, while the two figures on the right flee in terror.

Right: Detail of the sarcophagus of Laris Pulena *(early second century BC; Museo Nazionale, Tarquinia). The figure is that of an infernal demon wielding a hammer.*

Left: Alabaster urn in the hypogeum of the Volumni near Perugia (circa 200 BC). In the centre of the base on which the urn stands is a painted door representing the other world, and on the other side of it are two seated furies.

Epilogue: The Problem of Origins

Now that we have come to the end of this brief survey of Etruscan culture, perhaps a few conclusions can be drawn.

The problem most frequently dealt with nowadays in popular books on the Etruscans is the question of their origins; but the only brief reference to the matter in this book was in the chapter on language. My own view is that the question of Etruscan origins is not a matter of great importance today in the study of Etruscan civilization in historical times. The problem really arose with the Humanists, whose interest in the classical world caused attention to be drawn to the divided opinions of classical texts on this matter.

Herodotus, who lived in the fifth century BC, had collected a story in Ionia according to which the Tyrrhenoi, or Tyrsenoi, had emigrated from Lydia shortly after the Trojan War, under the leadership of the king's son, Tyrsenos (*Histories*, I, 94). Hellanicus, on the other hand, a contemporary of Herodotus, thought the Etruscans were Pelasgians, a mythical nomadic Greek people from Thessaly who, according to Anticlides (a third-century historian), reached Italy under the leadership of Tyrsenos after colonizing the Aegean islands of Lemnos and Imbros. This tradition appears in different forms in the writings of other ancient historians, and only Dionysius of Halicarnassus, who lived in Rome in early Imperial times, contradicts it (I, 25–30). He claims that the Etruscans were indigenous to Italy, and he criticizes Herodotus' idea and the whole tradition which derives from it.

These contrasting opinions are more or less irreconcilable, and until archaeological and linguistic evidence became available, it was simply a question of accepting one explanation or the other. But when the interpretation of archaeological evidence began to be applied to the debate, a third theory came into being, which held that the Etruscans were migrants from the north. This theory was popular amongst positivist archaeologists of the early twentieth century. The trouble was that there was a mistaken tendency to equate archaeological and ethnic factors, and it took Massimo Pallottino to set the matter straight in 1947. As he pointed out, the problem of a people's 'origins' in a historical sense must inevitably be expressed in terms of their cultural development. To take the example of two modern states, there would be no point in seeking a precise answer to the question: where did the French, or the English, come from? It would be pointless to wonder whether the French had Latin or Franco-Germanic

Above: Impasto urn from Cerveteri (early Iron Age; Museo Archeologico, Cerveteri). This image reflects the warlike and egalitarian nature of village society before contact was made with the culture of Greek and eastern merchants.

Right: Oriental faience vase from Tarquinia (end of the eighth century BC; Museo Nazionale, Tarquinia). This famous object is one of the many imports from the east which reached Etruria in the seventh century BC. It was found in a tomb dating to the early Orientalizing period. The upper frieze shows a cult ceremony being performed by the Pharaoh Bokenranf, whose name appears in hieroglyphs in the cartouche. Bokenranf (Bocchoris) reigned at Sais from 720 to 715 BC.

origins, or whether the English were originally Anglo-Saxon or Norman. The only possible solution to such problems must be in terms of the historical development of ethnic and political groups, whose very language is itself the result of the struggles and successes of their various component parts.

Hence the possible importance of the similarity between Etruscan and Lemnian mentioned earlier (see page 74), and also the need to push any possible migration of Etruscans from Asia Minor back into prehistory. Some weight must also be given to evidence from Egyptian sources, for there are inscriptions which commemorate the arrival across the sea of peoples who attacked the Egyptian Empire in the thirteenth century BC. Some of the many names mentioned are unidentifiable, but one notices the *Jqjwš.w* and the *Trš.w* ('Turuscia'), who have been identified by some – though in the face of objections – as the *Tyrsenoi* or Tyrrhenians. It is claimed that they were involved with other eastern peoples in the invasion of the Egyptian Empire which was subsequently repelled by Pharaoh Rameses II.

In the end, however, the problem of the origins of the Etruscans has to be seen primarily in terms of the attitudes of ancient historians. The oldest tradition is that of their Lydian origin, as set down by Herodotus and subsequently overlaid with 'Pelasgian' theories; whereas Dionysius of Halicarnassus takes up a position which accords well with the fairly clear view of ethnic matters which one might expect to find in Imperial Rome. Dionysius of Halicarnassus does not claim any particular merit for the Etruscans as a result of their indigenous origin, for he stresses the part played by the Greeks in the history of the peoples of ancient Italy, and in the development of Rome itself. He is not trying to establish a theory more in accordance with the facts, but to deny to the Etruscans the kind of high-class pedigree which current Lydian or Pelasgian theories provided, to the detriment of Rome and the Latins, whose ancestors were, according to him, of Greek origin.

An attempt has been made in this book to show that Etruscan problems need to be tackled in a different way nowadays. A vital consideration in present-day discussions is the process by which the culture of communities in Tuscany and Latium was modified by contact with the world of Greece, without a sense of ethnic identity being lost. In our own day, western culture is attempting to dominate the cultures of countries which are technologically less advanced, in a way which may make us ponder on the development of Etruscan civilization from its tribal stage in the Iron Age to its later urban form. Is this not a typical case of an indigenous culture adapting itself to an extraneous one, particularly under the stimulus of a later ruling class which deliberately took advantage of what the Greek world had to offer?

Archaeological evidence shows that Etruscan culture at this stage had a lasting high regard for the Greek world and accepted much of what it had to offer, although once political institutions had become firmly established, the Etruscans also began to compete with the Greeks. This meant that the Etruscans played a more valuable role amongst the nations involved in the broader area of Mediterranean history than did the Romans later on, when their imperialistic expansionism completely wiped out Etruscan culture, with the more or less open complicity of the new romanized Etruscan ruling class.

Chronology

Greece

Rise of the city-states and beginning of colonizing activities in the east

775   Greek trading post on Ischia

750   Foundation of Cumae

734/3   Foundation of Syracuse

650   Demaratus of Corinth settles at Tarquinia

540   Caeretans and Carthaginians defeat the Phocaeans at the Battle of the Sardinian Sea

504   Aristodemus, tyrant of Cumae, and the Latins defeat a son of Porsenna at Ariccia

474   Naval battle of Cumae: the fleet of Syracuse defeats that of the Etruscans

454/3   Syracusan expeditions against the mineral-rich regions of Etruria

384   Dionysius of Syracuse sacks the sanctuary at Pyrgi

272   The city of Taranto becomes an ally of Rome

241   Sicily becomes a Roman province

Etruria

Proto-Villanovan

Settlements in the Fiora valley, on the Tolfa Mountains and on Monte Cetona

Development of pre-urban communities

Villanovan

First contacts with Mediterranean maritime trade

(Phoenicians, Euboeans)

Orientalizing

(Corinthians)

Lucius Tarquinius in Rome

Urban Civilization

580   Greek trading post at Gravisca

Emilia and Campania colonized

Porsenna goes to Rome

Thefarie Velianas 'King' of Caere

413   The Etruscans join in the siege of Syracuse on the side of the Athenians

396   Destruction of the Veii

390

Slaves' revolt at Arezzo

353   Caere becomes a *Civitas sine suffragio* (i.e. a city without voting rights at Roman assemblies)

301   Slaves' revolt at Arezzo
Slaves' revolts at Volsinii, Oinarea and Roselle

264   Destruction of Volsinii

248   Destruction of Falerii

205   The Etruscans assist Scipio's fleet against Carthage

196   Slaves' revolt in Etruria

91   The Etruscans in Rome oppose the agrarian laws and the granting of citizenship to the Italic peoples

Rome

Burials in the Forum

814/3   Foundation of Rome (Timaeus)

Settlement on the Palatine

754/3   Foundation of Rome (Varro)

Forum paved

616   Etruscan dynasty begins

578   The reforms of Servius Tullius *(Macstrna)*

509   Fall of the Etruscan monarchy
Beginning of the Republic. Consuls of Etruscan origin recorded in the *Fasti* until 486

508   First commercial treaty between Rome and Carthage

The Gauls invade Italy

367/6   Licinian Rogations (give plebeians the same rights as patricians)

311, 309, 301, 298, 295, 281 Triumphs over the Etruscans

280   Triumphs over Volsinii and Vulci
Statonia made a *praefectura*
Roman colonies in Etruria:
278   Cosa
        Pyrgi
264   Castrum Novum

247   Alsium
245   Fregenae

183   Saturnia
181   Gravisca

90/88   Social War

Peninsular Italy unified

Prehistory

Prehistory covers the entire span of human development before written records. It begins and ends at different times in different places. In Greece it was around 1000 to 600 BC, and in Italy several centuries later. In most of northern and western Europe, prehistory lasted until the Roman Empire or later.

Proto-history

Past societies are described as 'Proto-historic' when they were themselves illiterate, but were in contact with literate neighbours.

Archaic History

This term normally refers to the oldest recorded history of a particular civilization.

Ancient History

This is a general description of the histories of the nations of the 'Classical' world – Greece and Rome. The timespan covered is approximately from the ninth century BC, the time of the Homeric poems, to the fall of Rome in the fifth century AD.

The Bronze Age and the Iron Age

In the Three Age system of the northern antiquaries, the Bronze Age was the first metal-using epoch, preceded by the Stone Age and followed by the Iron Age. The earliest use of bronze can be traced in south-eastern Europe in the later fifth millennium BC. The working of iron was introduced, probably from Asia Minor, into south-eastern Europe around 1000 BC, and into central Europe by the eighth-seventh centuries BC.

Bibliography

General Works

Banti, L. *Il mondo degli Etruschi*, Rome, 1969 (English translation: *The Etruscan Cities and their Culture*, London, 1973)

Bandinelli, R. Bianchi and Giuliano, A. *Les Étrusques et l'Italie avant Rome*, Paris, 1973

Heurgon, J. *La vie quotidienne chez les Étrusques,* Paris, 1961 (English translation: *Daily Life of the Etruscans*, London, 1964)

Macnamara, E. *Everyday Life of the Etruscans*, London, 1973

Pallottino, M. *Civiltà artistica etrusco-italica*, Florence, 1971

Pallottino, M. *Etruscologia*, Milan, 1973 (English translation: *The Etruscans*, Harmondsworth, 1975)

Popoli e civiltà dell'Italia antica, 1–6, Rome, 1973–1977

Scullard, H. H. *The Etruscan Cities and Rome*, London, 1967

Exhibition Catalogues

Mostra dell'arte e della civiltà etrusca, Milan, 1955

Mostra dell'Etruria padana e della città di Spina, Bologna, 1960

Arte e civiltà degli Etruschi, Turin, 1967

Masterpieces of Etruscan Art, Worcester Art Museum, 1967

Nuove letture di monumenti etruschi, Florence, 1971

Nuove scoperte e acquisizioni nell'Etruria meridionale, Rome, 1975

Civiltà del Lazio primitivo, Rome, 1976

Selected recent works on individual topics

The History of Etruscan Lands and Settlements

Aspetti e problemi dell'Etruria interna (Acts of the VIII Congress of Etruscan and Italic Studies, Orvieto, 1972), Florence, 1974

Atti del primo simposio internazionale di protostoria italiana, Orvieto, 1968 (Acts of the First International Symposium on Italian Proto-History), Rome, 1969

Colonna, G. 'L'Etruria meridionale interna dal villanoviano alle tombe rupestri' in *Studi Etruschi*, 35, 1967, p. 3ff.

Colonna, G. 'Ricerche sull'Etruria interna volsiniese' in *Studi Etruschi*, 41, 1973, p. 45ff.

Coppa, M. *Storia dell'urbanistica dalle origini all'ellenismo*, Turin, 1968, pp. 915–71

Cristofani, M. *Città e campagna nell'Etruria settentrionale*, Arezzo, 1976

Cristofani, M. 'Strutture insediative e modi di produzione' in *Caratteri dell'ellenismo nelle urne etrusche* (Acts of a Colloquium, Siena, 1976), Florence, 1977, p. 74ff.

Harris, W. V. *Rome in Etruria and Umbria*, Oxford, 1971

Heurgon, J. *Rome et la Méditerranée Occidentale jusqu'aux guerres puniques*, Paris, 1969 (English translation: *The Rise of Rome to 264 BC*, London, 1973)

'La città antica in Italia' in *Atti del Ce.S.D.I.R.*, 3, Milan, 1970–71

La città etrusca e italica preromana (Acts of a Congress, Bologna, 1965), Bologna, 1970

La civiltà arcaica di Vulci e la sua espansione (Acts of the X Congress of Etruscan and Italic Studies, Grosseto, 1975), Florence, 1977

Les origines de la république romaine (Fondation Hardt, *Entretiens sur l'antiquité classique*, XIII), Geneva, 1967

Mansuelli, G. A. 'Problemi e prospettive di studio sull'urbanistica antica. La città etrusca' in *Studi storici*, 8, 1967, p. 5ff.

Mansuelli, G. A. 'Marzabotto. Dix années de fouilles et recherches' in *Mélanges de l'Ecole française à Rome. Antiquité*, 84, 1972, p. 111ff.

Oestenberg, C. E. *Case etrusche ad Acquarossa*, Rome, 1975

Ogilvie, R. M. *Early Rome and the Etruscans*, London, 1977

Pallottino, M. 'Les origines des villes protohistoriques de l'Italie centrale' in *Miedzynarodowy Kongres Archeologii Slovensky*, IV, 1968, p. 253ff.

Pallottino, M. 'Le origini di Roma' in *Aufstieg und Niedergang der römischen Welt*, I, 1, Berlin – New York, 1972, p. 22ff.

Prayon, F. *Frühetruskische Grab- und Hausarchitektur*, Heidelberg, 1975

Schmiedt, G. *Atlante aerofotografico delle sedi umane in Italia*, II, *Le sedi scomparse*, Florence, 1970

Studies in the Romanization of Etruria (Acta Instituti Romani Finlandiae, V), Rome, 1975

Uggeri, G. and Uggeri Patitucci, S. 'Topografia e urbanistica di Spina' in *Studi Etruschi*, 42, 1974, p. 69ff.

Social Hierarchies and Classes

Ampolo, C. 'Su alcuni mutamenti sociali in Etruria e nel Lazio fra l'VIII e il V secolo a.C.' in *Dialoghi di archeologia*, 4–5, 1970–71, p. 37ff.

Colonna, G. 'Nome, gentilizio e società' in *Studi Etruschi*, 45, 1977, p. 175ff.

Cristofani, M. 'La tomba del Tifone, Cultura e società di Tarquinia in età tardoetrusca' in *Memorie dell'Accademia dei Lincei*, VIII. XIV.4, 1969, p. 213ff.

Heurgon, J. 'Classes et ordres chez les Étrusques' in *Recherches sur les structures sociales dans l'antiquité classique*, Paris, 1970, p. 19ff.

Lambrechts, R. *Essai sur les magistratures des républiques étrusques*, Brussels, 1959

Liou, B. *Praetores Etruriae XV populorum*, Brussels, 1969

Mazzarino, S. 'Sociologia del mondo etrusco e della tarda etruschità' in *Historia*, 6, 1957, p. 98ff.

Mazzarino, S. 'Le droit des Étrusques' in *Iura*, 12, 1961, p. 24ff.

Olzscha, K. 'Etruskisch *lautn* und *etera*' in *Glotta*, 46, 1968, p. 212ff.

Rix, H. 'Zur Ursprung des römisch-mittelitalischen Gentilnamsystems' in *Aufstieg und Niedergang der römischen Welt*, I, 2, Berlin-New York, 1972, p. 700ff.

Rix, H. 'L'apporto dell'onomastica alla storia sociale' in *Caratteri dell'ellenismo nelle urne etrusche* (Acts of a Colloquium, Siena, 1976), Florence, 1977, p. 64ff.

Štaerman, E. M. *Die Blütezeit der Sklavenwirtschaft in der römischen Republik*, Wiesbaden, 1969

Torelli, M. 'Tre studi di storia etrusca' in *Dialoghi di archeologia*, 8, 1974–5, p. 3ff.

Arts and Crafts and the Circulation of their Products

Ampolo, C. 'Servius rex signavit aes' in *La parola del passato*, 28, 1974, p. 382ff.

Beazley, J. D. *Etruscan Vase Painting*, Oxford, 1947

Becatti, G. *Oreficerie antiche dalle minoiche alle barbariche*, Rome, 1955

Boardman, J. *Greek Gems and Finger Rings*, London, 1970

Boardman, J. *The Greeks Overseas*, Harmondsworth, 1974

Boethius, A. and Ward Perkins, J. B. *Etruscan and Roman Architecture*, Harmondsworth, 1970

Bonfante, L. *Etruscan Dress*, Baltimore, 1975

Camporeale, G. *I commerci di Vetulonia in età orientalizzante*, Florence, 1968

Caratteri dell'ellenismo nelle urne etrusche (Acts of a Colloquium, Siena, 1976), Florence, 1977

Colonna, G. '"Firme" arcaiche di artefici nell'Italia centrale' in *Römische Mitteilungen*, 82, 1975, p. 181ff.

Cristofani, M. 'Il "dono" nell'Etruria arcaica' in *La parola del passato*, 30, 1975, p. 132ff.

Cristofani, M. 'Storia dell'arte e acculturazione: le pitture tombali arcaiche di Tarquinia' in *Prospettiva*, 7, 1976, p. 181ff.

Del Chiaro, M. *Etruscan Red-Figured Vase Painting at Caere*, Berkeley-Los Angeles, 1974

de Simone, C. 'Per la storia degli imprestiti greci in etrusco' in *Aufstieg und Niedergang der römischen Welt*, I, 2, Berlin-New York, 1972, p. 490ff.

Giuliano, A. 'Il pittore delle Rondini' in *Prospettiva*, 3, 1975, p. 4ff.

Gras, P. 'La piraterie tyrrhenienne en Mer Egée' in *L'Italie préromaine et la Rome républicaine*, Rome, 1976, p. 341ff.

Hemelrjik, J. M. *De Caeretanse Hydriae*, Rotterdam, 1957

Hus, A. *Recherches sur la statuaire en pierre étrusque archaïque*, Paris, 1961

Hus, A. *Les bronzes étrusques*, Brussels, 1975

'Incontro di studi sugli inizi della colonizzazione greca in Occidente' in *Dialoghi di archeologia*, 3, 1969

Introduzione alla numismatica etrusca (Acts of a Congress, Naples, 1974), supplement to vol. 22 of *Annali dell'Istituto Italiano di Numismatica*, Naples, 1975

Lambrechts, R. *Les inscriptions avec le mot 'tular' et le bornage étrusque*, Florence, 1970

Martelli, M. 'Documenti di arte orientalizzante da Chiusi' in *Studi Etruschi*, 41, 1973, p. 73ff.

Martelli, M. 'Un aspetto del commercio di manufatti artistici nel IV secolo a.C.: i sarcofagi in marmo' in *Prospettiva*, 3, 1975, p. 9ff.

Papasogli, G. *L'agricoltura degli Etruschi e dei Romani*, Rome, 1942

Peroni, R. 'Per uno studio dell'economia di scambio in Italia nel quadro ambientale dei secoli intorno al Mille a.C.' in *La parola del passato*, 26, 1969, p. 134ff.

Rebuffat-Emmanuel, D. *Le miroir étrusque*, Paris, 1973

Strøm, I. *Problems Concerning the Origin and Early Development of the Etruscan Orientalizing Style*, Odense, 1971

Szilàgyi, J. G. *Etrusko-Korinthosi Vàzafestészet*, Budapest, 1975

Torelli, M. 'Beziehungen zwischen Griechen und Etruskern im 5. und 4. Jahrh. v.u.Z.' in *Hellenische Poleis*, II, Berlin, 1973, p. 823ff.

Zazoff, P. *Etruskische Skarabäen*, Mainz am Rhein, 1968

Religious Life and Culture

Bloch, R. *Les prodiges dans l'antiquité (Grèce, Etrurie, Rome)*, Paris, 1963

Camporeale, G. 'Saghe greche nell'arte etrusca arcaica' in *La parola del passato*, 19, 1964, p. 428ff.

Colonna, G. 'Scriba cum rege sedens' in *L'Italie préromaine et la Rome républicaine*, Rome, 1976, p. 187ff.

Cristofani, M. 'Origine e diffusione dell'alfabeto etrusco' in *Aufstieg und Niedergang der römischen Welt*, I, 2, Berlin-New York, 1972, p. 466ff.

Cristofani, M. *Introduzione allo studio dell'etrusco*, Florence, 1973

Dumézil, P. *La religion romaine archaïque*, Paris, 1966 (English translation: *Archaic Roman Religion*, London, 1970)

Giglioli, G. Q. 'La religione degli Etruschi', with a note by G. Camporeale, in P. Tacchi Venturi, *Storia delle Religioni*, 6th ed., Turin, 1971, II, p. 539ff.

Hampe, R. and Simon, E. *Griechischen Sagen in der frühen etruskischen Kunst*, Mainz am Rhein, 1964

Herbig, Rh. and Simon, E. *Götter und Dämonen der Etrusker*, Mainz am Rhein, 1965

Le lamine di Pyrgi, Accademia Nazionale dei Lincei, Quaderno no. 147, Rome, 1970

L'etrusco arcaico (Acts of a Colloquium, Florence, 1974), Florence, 1976

Mavleyev, E. V. 'The "book of life" of the Etruscans' (in Russian) in *Trudi Gosudarstvennogo Ermitagia*, 17, 1976, p. 87ff.

Pallottino, M. 'Sulla lettura e sul contenuto della grande iscrizione di Capua' in *Studi Etruschi*, 20, 1948–9, p. 159ff.

Pallottino, M. 'La lingua degli Etruschi' in *Popoli e civiltà dell'Italia antica*, 6, Rome, 1977

Pfiffig, A. J. *Religio etrusca*, Graz, 1975

Torelli, M. *Elogia Tarquiniensia*, Florence, 1975

Weinstock, S. 'Libri Fulgurales' in *Papers of the British School at Rome*, 19, 1971, p. 122ff.

The Problem of Etruscan Origins

Aigner Foresti, L. *Tesi, ipotesi e considerazioni sull'origine degli Etruschi*, Graz, 1974

Hencken, H. *Tarquinia and Etruscan Origins*, London, 1968

Musti, D. 'Tendenze nella storiografia romana e greca su Roma arcaica' in *Quaderni Urbinati di cultura classica*, 10, Rome, 1970

Pallottino, M. *L'origine degli Etruschi*, Rome, 1947

Pallottino, M. 'Nuovi studi sul problema delle origini etrusche (bilancio critico)' in *Studi Etruschi*, 29, 1961, p. 3ff.

Index

Page references to photographs are printed in bold.